Items should be returned on or before the last date shown below. Items not already requested by other borrowers may be renewed in person, in writing or by telephone. To renew, please quote the number on the barcode label. To renew online a PIN is required. This can be requested at your local library.
Renew online @ **www.dublincitypubliclibraries.ie**
Fines charged for overdue items will include postage incurred in recovery. Damage to or loss of items will be charged to the borrower.

Leabharlanna Poiblí Chathair Bhaile Átha Cliath
Dublin City Public Libraries

Baile Átha Cliath
Dublin City

Date Due	Date Due	Date Due

2 1 APR 2015

1 4 OCT 2016

D1494422

To my late mother, Dorcas Ryan, and late father, Gerry Ryan. Mam you raised us after Dad died – this is for you with love.

To Mary O'Shaughnessy (Mum number two!). Your high standards have finally rubbed off on me.

MERCIER PRESS
Cork
www.mercierpress.ie

© Eddie Ryan, 2014

ISBN: 978 1 78117 289 6

10 9 8 7 6 5 4 3 2 1

A CIP record for this title is available from the British Library.

Printed and bound in the EU.

CONTENTS

ACKNOWLEDGEMENTS

To Phil Murphy, editor of *Ireland's Own*: thanks for everything Phil, have a great retirement.

Thanks to Catherine Moloney: you taught me that patience is a virtue!

Thanks also to my publisher Mercier Press, and to Sarah and Wendy for their fantastic support in guiding me through the 'perils' of writing my first book.

Dedicated to GAA players the world over.

ALL-IRELAND SENIOR HURLING & FOOTBALL CHAMPIONSHIP FACTS

SENIOR HURLING

- The All-Ireland Senior Hurling Championship final was listed in second place by broadcasting giant CNN in its '10 sporting events you have to see live', after the Olympic Games and ahead of both the FIFA World Cup and UEFA European Football Championship.

- Hurling is the oldest field sport in the world, with records dating back to seventh- and eighth-century AD Irish laws.

- The first All-Ireland Hurling Championship took place in 1887, with only five teams participating.

- Tommy Healy of Coolcroo in Tipperary scored the first ever goal in an All-Ireland hurling final.

- Kerry won their first and only All-Ireland hurling final in 1891.

- Inter-county teams replaced club teams in 1892. Up to that point counties had been represented by club sides.

- Tipperary (including clubs representing Tipperary) appeared in eight finals between 1887 and 1908, winning on every occasion. Kilkenny ended that remarkable run in 1909, on a 4–6 to 0–12 scoreline.

– Kilkenny lost their first four All-Ireland finals to Cork, Tipperary, Limerick and Tipperary again, in that order.

– In 1924 Mick Gill created history by winning two All-Ireland senior hurling medals in the same year and for different counties. In September he played on the Galway side which beat Limerick in the delayed 1923 final. In the 1924 final he played on the victorious Dublin team, which beat his old team, Galway.

– The All-Ireland final of 1931 between Cork and Kilkenny had to be played three times before Cork finally landed the spoils.

– The 1939 All-Ireland final is remembered as 'the Thunder and Lightning final'. On the eve of the outbreak of the Second World War, Cork and Kilkenny played out an epic contest. Thunder and lightning greeted the players' arrival at the start of the second half. Victory eventually went to the Kilkenny men, by a single point.

– In 1944 Cork became the first team to win four All-Ireland hurling titles in a row.

– The 1956 All-Ireland final between Cork and Wexford drew a record hurling crowd of 84,856.

– On the one-hundredth birthday of the All-Ireland Senior Hurling Championship in 1987, Galway beat Kilkenny.

– The All-Ireland hurling final of 1993 was the last game to be played in the old Croke Park before the demolition of the Cusack Stand and the start of a multimillion pound redevelopment of the entire stadium.

- The All-Ireland final of 1994 will forever be remembered as the 'five-minute final'. Up to the last five minutes of play, Limerick looked set to end a wait of over twenty years and win their first All-Ireland title since 1973. However, Offaly staged one of the greatest comebacks of all time, scoring two goals and five points in the last few minutes of the game to win 3–16 to 2–13.

- The championship of 1997 saw the introduction of the so-called 'back-door' system, whereby the beaten provincial finalists from Munster and Leinster are allowed to contest the All-Ireland series.

- Tipperary and Clare contested the final in 1997, making it the first all-Munster All-Ireland final.

- In the All-Ireland semi-final replay of 1998 between Clare and Offaly, referee Jimmy Cooney blew the whistle two minutes early. The Offaly team, who were trailing at the time, launched a sit-down protest on the pitch, where they were joined by their irate supporters. A replay was granted after this protest, which Offaly won.

- The All-Ireland final on 11 September 2005 was the first to be played at the fully refurbished Croke Park. The Cusack Stand, the Canal Stand, the Hogan

Stand and the new Hill 16 and Nally End have a total capacity of 82,300.

- In 2009 Kilkenny equalled Cork's historic achievement by winning their fourth All-Ireland title in a row. They defeated a determined Tipperary, courtesy of a late Henry Shefflin penalty.

- The 2013 All-Ireland hurling final was the first to be played under floodlights. This happened exactly 100 years after the Croke Park site was first purchased.

- The 'big three' – Tipperary, Kilkenny and Cork – account for the most All-Ireland's won. Between them they have won 90 out of 126 titles contested, over 70 per cent.

- No Ulster team has ever won an All-Ireland Senior Hurling Championship, although Antrim have reached two finals (1943 and 1989).

- Jack Lynch is the only player in GAA history to have won six successive All-Ireland medals (five were for hurling, one for football).

- Tipperary net minder Brendan Cummins holds the all-time championship appearance record, lining out seventy-three times in the famous blue and gold.

- Three Kilkenny players hold the record for the number of All-Ireland senior hurling medals won. Full-back Noel Hickey, goalie Noel Skehan (3 as a sub) and Henry Shefflin hold a record nine medals.

Shefflin is, however, the only one who played in all of the nine finals he received a medal for.

- Galway have reached twenty-two All-Ireland finals and lost eighteen.

- Kilkenny have reached the most All-Ireland finals, fifty-nine in total.

- Kilkenny have also lost the most finals (25), and won the most (34).

Scoring Records

- Eddie Keher of Kilkenny is one of the most prolific marksmen in GAA history. In 1959 he lined out in both Senior and Minor All-Ireland hurling finals. In a total of fifty championship appearances between 1959 and 1977 he scored thirty-five goals and 334 points. Not only that, but Keher also set and broke a number of individual records. In the 1963 All-Ireland final, Keher amassed a total of fourteen points. In the 1971 All-Ireland final against Tipperary, he scored a remarkable tally of 2–11. Despite Keher's heroics, the 'Cats' were beaten by Tipperary. He is the second highest scorer of all time, behind fellow Kilkenny great Henry Shefflin.

- The highest total recorded by a player in a final is held by Tipperary legend Nicky English. The man from Lattin-Cullen scored two goals and twelve points against an unfortunate Antrim in 1989.

- Nicky Rackard of Wexford scored the highest total in a championship match. In Wexford's 12–17 to 2–3 defeat of Ulster representative Antrim in the 1954 All-Ireland semi-final, he scored seven goals and seven points. His tally of six goals and four points against Dublin is also another scoring record. The prolific Rackard also scored five goals and four points against Galway in the 1956 All-Ireland semi-final.

- Before the 1930s scoring records for championship games were rarely kept, but a number of players have been credited with enormous scoring tallies:

  > Andy 'Dooric' Buckley scored at least six goals when Cork beat Kilkenny by 8–9 to 0–8 in the 1903 All-Ireland 'home' final. Other news reports credit him with seven goals and four points.

  > P. J. Riordan is reported to have gone on a scoring blitz and scored all but a solitary point of Tipperary's total when they beat Kilkenny by 6–8 to 0–1 in the 1895 All-Ireland final.

  > Jimmy Kelly of Kilkenny has gone down in legend as having scored seven goals in thirty minutes against Cork in the replay of the 1905 final.

Top Scorers All-Ireland Senior Hurling Championship (championship scores only)

Henry Shefflin, Kilkenny: 27–484 (565 pts), 68 games, 1999–present. Average points per game (ppg): 8.3.

Eddie Keher, Kilkenny: 35–334 (439 pts), 50 games, 1959–77. Average ppg: 8.78.

Eoin Kelly, Tipperary: 21–369 (432 pts), 60 games, 2000–present. Average ppg: 7.2.

Christy Ring, Cork: 33–208 (307 pts), 64 games, 1940–63. Average ppg: 4.8.

D. J. Carey, Kilkenny: 34–195 (297 pts), 57 games, 1989–2005. Average ppg: 5.2.

Nicky Rackard, Wexford: 59–96 (273 pts), 36 games, 1940–57. Average ppg: 7.6.

Joe Deane, Cork: 10–239 (269 pts), 50 games, 1996–2008. Average ppg: 5.4.

Niall Gilligan, Clare: 20–197 (257 pts), 56 games, 1997–2009. Average ppg: 4.6.

Paul Flynn, Waterford: 24–181 (253 pts), 45 games, 1993–2008. Average ppg: 5.6.

Ben O'Connor, Cork: 8–224 (248 pts), 52 games, 1999–2011. Average ppg: 4.8.

Roll of Honour*

Kilkenny (34): 1904, 1905, 1907, 1909, 1911, 1912, 1913, 1922, 1932, 1933, 1935, 1939, 1947, 1957, 1963, 1967, 1969, 1972, 1974, 1975, 1979, 1982, 1983, 1992,

1993, 2000, 2002, 2003, 2006, 2007, 2008, 2009, 2011, 2012

Cork (30): 1890, 1892, 1893, 1894, 1902, 1903, 1919, 1926, 1928, 1929, 1931, 1941, 1942, 1943, 1944, 1946, 1952, 1953, 1954, 1966, 1970, 1976, 1977, 1978, 1984, 1986, 1990, 1999, 2004, 2005

Tipperary (26): 1887, 1895, 1896, 1898, 1899, 1900, 1906, 1908, 1916, 1925, 1930, 1937, 1945, 1949, 1950, 1951, 1958, 1961, 1962, 1964, 1965, 1971, 1989, 1991, 2001, 2010

Limerick (7): 1897, 1918, 1921, 1934, 1936, 1940, 1973

Dublin (6): 1889, 1917, 1920, 1924, 1927, 1938

Wexford (6): 1910, 1955, 1956, 1960, 1968, 1996

Galway (4): 1923, 1980, 1987, 1988

Offaly (4): 1981, 1985, 1994, 1998

Clare (4): 1914, 1995, 1997, 2013

Waterford (2): 1948, 1959

Kerry (1): 1891

London (1): 1901

Laois (1): 1915

* not contested in 1888

SENIOR FOOTBALL

- The first final was between Commercials of Limerick and Young Irelands of Louth. The teams consisted of twenty-one players a side. The final was played in Beech Hill, Clonskeagh, with Commercials winning by 1–4 to 0–3. Young Ireland's are still in existence today, making them one of the oldest GAA clubs in the country, as they were formed in 1884.

- The second championship remained unfinished owing to the American Invasion Tour (see Reeling in the GAA Years). The 1888 provincial champion-ships had been completed (Tipperary, Kilkenny and Monaghan winning them; no Connacht teams entered) but the GAA elected not to finish the com-petition.

- In 1892 inter-county teams were introduced to the All-Ireland Championship, replacing club sides. The rules of hurling and football were also altered. Goals were made equal to five points, and teams were reduced from twenty-one to seventeen a side.

- The 1910 final was awarded to Louth. Their oppos-ing team, Kerry, refused to travel to play in the final as the Great Southern and Western Railway would not sell tickets to their fans at reduced rates.

- In 1913 GAA teams are reduced to fifteen players from seventeen. Kerry won the first fifteen-a-side football final defeating Wexford by 2–2 to 0–3.

- London were one of the first powerhouses of Gaelic football and reached the final four times in the early years of the competition.

- The championship has never been won by a team from outside Ireland, though London have played in a total of five finals.

- Galway were the first team from Connacht to win an All-Ireland title, doing so in 1925.

- In 1933 Cavan became the first team from Ulster to win an All-Ireland title. However, the county has not contested the big one in over sixty years. Its last appearance was in the 1952 decider against Meath.

- Mayo, who last won in 1951, have now contested a further seven finals without tasting victory.

- The 1961 final between Down and Offaly set the attendance record with a crowd of 90,556 spectators.

- Garry McMahon's goal for Kerry after thirty-four seconds in the 1962 All-Ireland senior football final is the fastest goal in the history of the competition.

- Two teams have won the All-Ireland Senior Football Championship as part of a double with that year's All-Ireland Senior Hurling Championship, namely Cork (1890 and 1990) and Tipperary (1895 and 1900).

- Kerry are the most successful football team in the All-Ireland Senior Football Championship. Their first win came in 1903 and they have been successful on thirty-six occasions. They have won four in a row twice (1929–32 and 1978–81), and twice been successful for three consecutive years (1939–41 and 1984–86).

- In 1943 Joe Stafford of Cavan made history by becoming the first player to be sent off in an All-Ireland senior football final.

- Dublin won an ill-tempered 1983 final with Galway, despite finishing the game with just twelve players. Three 'Dubs' and one Galwayman saw red during the decider. Brian Mullins was the first to receive his marching orders, followed by Ray Hazley, Tomás Tierney (Galway) and Ciaran Duff.

- The 1991, 1992, 1993 and 1994 finals were all won by Ulster teams – Down, Donegal, Derry and Down again. Donegal and Derry's wins were those counties first ever Sam Maguire triumphs.

- When Meath crossed swords with Down in the 1991 decider it was their tenth match of the championship. Four games against Dublin, which included three replays, were followed by two more against Wicklow. Further games with Offaly and Laois completed a marathon provincial campaign. 'The Royals' then defeated Roscommon, before finally succumbing to Down in the All-Ireland final.

- The All-Ireland qualifiers, or 'back-door' system as they have come to be known, were introduced in

2001. Later that year the final brought victory to Galway, who, despite losing to Roscommon in the Connacht semi-final, became the first football team to win an All-Ireland by emerging from 'the back door'.

– The 2003 final between Armagh and Tyrone was the first between two teams from the same province.

– Armagh won their first ever All-Ireland in 2002, defeating Kerry by a single point.

– In 2013 Hawk-Eye was introduced for championship matches at Croke Park only. This system was designed to remove ambiguity over whether or not a point had been scored. It was first used to confirm that Offaly substitute Peter Cunningham's attempted point had gone wide in the early minutes of the second half in a game against Kildare.

– 2013 brought the first Friday night encounter in the history of the championship, when the Leinster Championship first-round qualifier between Carlow and Laois was played on Friday 28 June.

– The brothers Spillane from Kerry – Pat, Tom and Mick – hold the record number of All-Ireland senior winners' medals in either hurling or football with nineteen in total. Including medals won as non-playing substitutes, Pat won eight, Tom seven and Mick four.

Roll of Honour*

Kerry (36): 1903, 1904, 1909, 1913, 1914, 1924, 1926, 1929, 1930, 1931, 1932, 1937, 1939, 1940, 1941, 1946, 1953, 1955, 1959, 1962, 1969, 1970, 1975, 1978, 1979, 1980, 1981, 1984, 1985, 1986, 1997, 2000, 2004, 2006, 2007, 2009

Dublin (24): 1891, 1892, 1894, 1897, 1898, 1899, 1901, 1902, 1906, 1907, 1908, 1921, 1922, 1923, 1942, 1958, 1963, 1974, 1976, 1977, 1983, 1995, 2011, 2013

Galway (9): 1925, 1934, 1938, 1956, 1964, 1965, 1966, 1998, 2001

Meath (7): 1949, 1954, 1967, 1987, 1988, 1996, 1999

Cork (7): 1890, 1911, 1945, 1973, 1989, 1990, 2010

Wexford (5): 1893, 1915, 1916, 1917, 1918

Cavan (5): 1933, 1935, 1947, 1948, 1952

Down (5): 1960, 1961, 1968, 1991, 1994

Tipperary (4): 1889, 1895, 1900, 1920

Kildare (4): 1905, 1919, 1927, 1928

Louth (3): 1910, 1912, 1957

Mayo (3): 1936, 1950, 1951

Offaly (3): 1971, 1972, 1982

Tyrone (3): 2003, 2005, 2008

Limerick (2): 1887, 1896

Roscommon (2): 1943, 1944

Donegal (2): 1992, 2012

Derry (1): 1993

Armagh (1): 2002

* not contested in 1888

GAA PRESIDENTS
AND GENERAL SECRETARIES

- Maurice Davin is the only man ever to serve two terms as president. He resigned on both occasions.

- E. M. Bennett of Clare is the shortest serving GAA president. His term lasted only two months. As the IRB-backed candidate his appointment was opposed by the non-political wing of the GAA and he was removed in January 1888.

- The longest serving president of the GAA was James Nowlan from Kilkenny. He served from 1901–21. After his death the GAA stadium in Kilkenny city was named in his honour.

- Former GAA President Patrick Breen from Wexford won two All-Ireland senior football medals with different counties (Wexford and Dublin).

- General Secretary Luke O'Toole from Wicklow (1901–29) is largely credited with the purchase of the Croke Park grounds in 1913.

- Aogán Ó Fearghail became the first Cavan man to be selected as president, at the 2014 GAA Congress. His term starts in 2015.

- The youngest president was Seán Ryan, a Tipperary native. He moved to Dublin and had a lifelong involvement with the GAA.

- Daniel McCarthy is the only Dublin-born man to serve as president (1921–24).

- Michael Deering, a native of Limerick, is to date the only president to die in office.

- Frank B. Dineen is the only person in GAA history to have served as both president and secretary.

LIST OF ALL GAA PRESIDENTS

Liam Ó Néill (Laois): 2012–15

Christy Cooney (Cork): 2009–12

Nickey Brennan (Kilkenny): 2006–09

Sean Kelly (Kerry): 2003–06

Sean McCague (Monaghan): 2000–03

Joe McDonagh (Galway): 1997–2000

Jack Boothman (Wicklow): 1994–97

Peter Quinn (Fermanagh): 1991–94

John Dowling (Offaly): 1988–91

Mick Loftus (Mayo): 1985–87

Paddy Buggy (Kilkenny): 1982–84

Paddy McFlynn (Down): 1979–82

Con Murphy (Cork): 1976–79

Donal Keenan (Roscommon): 1973–76

Pat Fanning (Waterford): 1970–73

Seamus Ó Riain (Tipperary): 1967–70

Alf Murray (Armagh): 1964–67

Hugh Byrne (Wicklow): 1961–64

J. J. Stuart (Dublin): 1958–61

Seamus McFerran (Antrim): 1955–58

M. V. O'Donoghue (Waterford): 1952–55

Michael Kehoe (Wexford): 1949–52

Dan O'Rourke (Roscommon): 1946–49

Seamus Gardiner (Tipperary): 1943–46

Padraig MacNamee (Antrim): 1938–43

Robert O'Keeffe (Laois): 1935–38

Seán McCarthy (Cork): 1932–35

Seán Ryan (Dublin): 1928–32

Liam Clifford (Limerick): 1926–28

Patrick Breen (Wexford): 1924–26

Daniel McCarthy (Dublin): 1921–24

James Nowlan (Kilkenny): 1901–21

Michael Deering (Cork): 1898–1901

Frank B. Dineen (Limerick): 1895–98

Peter J. Kelly (Galway): 1889–95

Maurice Davin (Tipperary): 1888

E. M. Bennett (Clare): 1887

Maurice Davin (Tipperary): 1884–87

LIST OF ALL GAA GENERAL SECRETARIES

Páraic Duffy (Monaghan): 2008–present

Liam Mulvihill (Longford): 1979–2007

Seán Ó Síocháin (Cork): 1964–79

Padraic Ó Caoimh (Cork): 1929–64

Luke O'Toole (Wicklow): 1901–29

Frank B. Dineen (Limerick): 1898–1901

Richard T. C. Blake (Meath): 1895–98

David Walsh (Clare): 1894–95

Patrick Tobin (Dublin): 1891–94

Maurice Moynihan (Kerry): 1890–92

P. R. Cleary (Limerick): 1889–90

William Prendergast (Tipperary): 1888–89

James Moore (Louth): 1887–88

Timothy O'Riordan (Cork): 1885–89

J. B. O'Reilly (Dublin): 1885–87

John Wyse Power (Kildare): 1884–87

John McKay (Cork): 1884–85

Michael Cusack (Clare): 1884–85

THE PROVINCIAL CHAMPIONSHIP

MUNSTER SENIOR HURLING CHAMPIONSHIP

- The provincial championship was first held in 1888.

- Between them Cork and Tipperary have won ninety-two Munster titles.

- When Clare beat Limerick in the 1995 Munster final it ended a wait of sixty-three years for a provincial title.

- The winning trophy is similar in design to the Liam MacCarthy Cup, but has no name.

- Kerry won their only Munster Senior Hurling title in 1891.

- In the 1935 semi-final, at the Thurles sports field, Tommy Kelly of Cork collided with a Limerick mid-fielder and was so badly injured he received the Last Rites.

- In all Galway made twelve appearances during a ten-year period spent in the Munster Championship, in which they played due to a lack of competition in Connacht. There is now no championship in Connacht and Galway play in the Leinster Championship.

- Galway defeated Clare in 1961 at the Gaelic Grounds. This was their first victory over their hurling neighbours and their only ever win in Munster.

- There have been two 'Munster' All-Ireland finals: Tipperary and Clare in 1979 and Clare and Cork in 2013.

- When Tipperary defeated Cork in 1987 it ended a sixteen-year famine for the 'Premier' men.

- In 1918 Limerick won the Munster title by a record thirty-one points, scoring 11–3 against a hapless Clare.

Roll of Honour

Cork (52): 1888, 1890, 1892, 1893, 1894, 1901, 1902, 1903, 1904, 1905, 1907, 1912, 1915, 1919, 1920, 1926, 1927, 1928, 1929, 1931, 1939, 1942, 1943, 1944, 1946, 1947, 1952, 1953, 1954, 1956, 1966, 1969, 1970, 1972, 1975, 1976, 1977, 1978, 1979, 1982, 1983, 1984, 1985, 1986, 1990, 1992, 1999, 2000, 2003, 2005, 2006, 2014

Tipperary (40): 1895, 1896, 1898, 1899, 1900, 1906, 1908, 1909, 1913, 1916, 1917, 1922, 1924, 1925, 1930, 1937, 1941, 1945, 1949, 1950, 1951, 1958, 1960, 1961, 1962, 1964, 1965, 1967, 1968, 1971, 1987, 1988, 1989, 1991, 1993, 2001, 2008, 2009, 2011, 2012

Limerick (19): 1897, 1910, 1911, 1918, 1921, 1923, 1933, 1934, 1935, 1936, 1940, 1955, 1973, 1974, 1980, 1981, 1994, 1996, 2013

Waterford (9): 1938, 1948, 1957, 1959, 1963, 2002, 2004, 2007, 2010

Clare (6): 1889, 1914, 1932, 1995, 1997, 1998

Kerry (1): 1891

LEINSTER SENIOR HURLING CHAMPIONSHIP

– Kilkenny have won sixty-nine Leinster Senior Hurling titles.

– Galway won their first Leinster title in 2012, defeating defending champions Kilkenny. In defeating the 'Cats', the Galway men brought their opponents' unbeaten championship run, which started in 2005, to an end.

– Michael Kavanagh of Kilkenny has a record thirteen winning Leinster medals.

– Westmeath reached their only final in 1937. They lost by eight points.

– Wexford won their first title in 1890, defeating Laois by 2–9 to 0–3.

– The Leinster Championship cup is named after Bob O'Keeffe, a native of Kilkenny who won an All-Ireland medal with Laois and served as president of the GAA in the 1930s.

– The 1929 championship was declared null and void. Kilkenny defeated Dublin, but both were disqualified after the match for turning up late for the final.

– Laois have only won three Leinster titles, two in a row in 1914 and 1915, and one in 1949.

– Antrim competed in the Leinster Championship for the first time in the preliminary round in 2009.

Roll of Honour

Kilkenny (69): 1888, 1893, 1895, 1897, 1898, 1900, 1903, 1904, 1905, 1907, 1909, 1911, 1912, 1913, 1916, 1922, 1923, 1925, 1926, 1931, 1932, 1933, 1935, 1936, 1937, 1939, 1940, 1943, 1945, 1946, 1947, 1950, 1953, 1957, 1958, 1959, 1963, 1964, 1966, 1967, 1969, 1971, 1972, 1973, 1974, 1975, 1978, 1979, 1982, 1983, 1986, 1987, 1991, 1992, 1993, 1998, 1999, 2000, 2001, 2002, 2003, 2005, 2006, 2007, 2008, 2009, 2010, 2011, 2014

Dublin (24): 1889, 1892, 1894, 1896, 1902, 1906, 1908, 1917, 1919, 1920, 1921, 1924, 1927, 1928, 1930, 1934, 1938, 1941, 1942, 1944, 1948, 1952, 1961, 2013

Wexford (20): 1890, 1891, 1899, 1901, 1910, 1918, 1951, 1954, 1955, 1956, 1960, 1962, 1965, 1968, 1970, 1976, 1977, 1996, 1997, 2004

Offaly (9): 1980, 1981, 1984, 1985, 1988, 1989, 1990, 1994, 1995

Laois (3): 1914, 1915, 1949

Galway (1): 2012

CONNACHT SENIOR HURLING CHAMPIONSHIP

– Galway were declared winners of the first championship in 1898 as they had no opponents and were representing Connacht in the All-Ireland series.

– Roscommon's win in the 1913 championship was their first and only victory.

– Galway's eleven-in-a-row bid came unstuck in

1909. Mayo scored 10–1 in total to secure a shock six-goal victory.

- Galway won their last Connacht title in 1999, beating Roscommon. There has been no Connacht Championship since.

- Galway defeated Roscommon in five finals in a row from 1995–99.

- Roscommon have contested nineteen deciders and lost eighteen of them.

- The only draw in a Connacht final occurred in 1916.

- Sligo contested their only final in 1900.

- Galway were declared champions from 2000 to 2008 as there were no other teams competing. In 2009 they were granted entry into the Leinster Championship, starting with a three-year trial period.

Roll of Honour*

Galway (25): 1900, 1901, 1902, 1903, 1904, 1905, 1906, 1907, 1908, 1910, 1911, 1912, 1914, 1915, 1917, 1919, 1920, 1921, 1922, 1994, 1995, 1996, 1997, 1998, 1999

Mayo (1): 1909

Roscommon (1): 1913

*not contested in 1918 or from 1923–93

ULSTER SENIOR HURLING CHAMPIONSHIP

– The competition was founded in 1900.

– The winners are presented with the Liam Harvey Cup.

– Down bridged a fifty-one year gap and caused a huge upset when they defeated Antrim in 1992.

– Gerald McGrattan played a starring role in Down's march to the title in 1992. An unknown at the start of the championship, he went on to become the county's first All-Star that year.

– New York compete in the Ulster Championship and reached the 2006 final, losing to Antrim.

– Armagh, better known for their football exploits, have reached two finals, their last in 2011.

– The Ulster Championship had a change of format in 2009. The winners no longer gained entry into All-Ireland Senior Hurling Championship proper.

– Antrim created history by winning two Provincial titles within the space of six months. They won the delayed 2013 Ulster title on 2 February 2014, defeating Down by 4–20 to 1–17. On Sunday 13 July they defeated Derry by 2–17 to 2–16, winning their thirteenth title in a row. Derry were the last team to defeat Antrim in an Ulster final, in 2001.

– Monaghan reached two finals in a row (1914 and 1915) winning on both occasions.

Roll of Honour*

Antrim (55): 1900, 1901, 1903, 1904, 1905, 1907, 1909, 1910, 1911, 1913, 1916, 1924, 1925, 1926, 1927, 1928, 1929, 1930, 1931, 1933, 1934, 1935, 1936, 1937, 1938, 1939, 1940, 1943, 1944, 1945, 1946, 1947, 1948, 1949, 1989, 1990, 1991, 1993, 1994, 1996, 1998, 1999, 2002, 2003, 2004, 2005, 2006, 2007, 2008, 2009, 2010, 2011, 2012, 2013, 2014

Derry (4): 1902, 1908, 2000, 2001

Down (4): 1941, 1992, 1995, 1997

Donegal (3): 1906, 1923, 1932

Monaghan (2): 1914, 1915

* not contested in 1912, 1917, 1918–22, 1942 and 1950–88

MUNSTER SENIOR FOOTBALL CHAMPIONSHIP

–   Tipperary side Bohercrowe won the first two Munster Championships, in 1888 and 1889.

–   In 1979 Kerry scored a whopping 9–21 (one of the highest scores ever recorded in a championship game) against Clare in a Munster Championship match that was dubbed 'The Milltown Massacre'.

–   Fitzgerald Stadium in Killarney is named after famous Kerry footballer Dick Fitzgerald. While the venue is famous for hosting Munster Senior Football finals, it also staged an All-Ireland hurling final between Tipperary and Kilkenny in 1937.

–   Clare caused the biggest upset in championship

history when they defeated red-hot favourites Kerry at Limerick's Gaelic Grounds in 1992, by 2–10 to 0–12. Kerry legends Jack O'Shea and Seamus Moynahan played their last games for Kerry in this shock defeat. That game also elicited the famous comment 'There won't be a cow milked in Clare tonight' from RTÉ correspondent Marty Morrissey.

– Kerry and Cork's dominance of the competition has only been broken by Tipperary in 1935 and Clare in 1992.

– Pat Spillane of Kerry has won a record twelve Munster medals in three different decades, the 1970s, 1980s and 1990s.

– Cork won their first title in 1890, and a century later in 1990 they won their twenty-eighth Munster crown.

Roll of Honour*

Kerry (76): 1892, 1903, 1904, 1905, 1908, 1909, 1910, 1912, 1913, 1914, 1915, 1919, 1923, 1924, 1925, 1926, 1927, 1929, 1930, 1931, 1932, 1933, 1934, 1936, 1937, 1938, 1939, 1940, 1941, 1942, 1944, 1946, 1947, 1948, 1950, 1951, 1953, 1954, 1955, 1958, 1959, 1960, 1961, 1962, 1963, 1964, 1965, 1968, 1969, 1970, 1972, 1975, 1976, 1977, 1978, 1979, 1980, 1981, 1982, 1984, 1985, 1986, 1991, 1996, 1997, 1998, 2000, 2001, 2003, 2004, 2005, 2007, 2010, 2011, 2013, 2014

Cork (37): 1890, 1891, 1893, 1894, 1897, 1899, 1901, 1906, 1907, 1911, 1916, 1928, 1943, 1945, 1949, 1952, 1956, 1957, 1966, 1967, 1971, 1973, 1974, 1983, 1987,

1988, 1989, 1990, 1993, 1994, 1995, 1999, 2002, 2006, 2008, 2009, 2012

Tipperary (9): 1888, 1889, 1895, 1900, 1902, 1918, 1920, 1922, 1935

Clare (2): 1917, 1992

Waterford (1): 1898

Limerick (1): 1896

* not contested in 1921

LEINSTER SENIOR FOOTBALL CHAMPIONSHIP

– Wexford and Dublin have won the most consecutive championships: Wexford between 1913 and 1918 and Dublin between 1974 and 1979.

– Wicklow have never won a Leinster Senior crown and they reached their only final in 1897.

– Dublin and Meath needed three replays to reach a decision in their first-round clash in 1991. The titanic battles captivated the nation. The sides were still level after 340 minutes of combat, but the outcome was finally decided by a late Meath point from David Beggy. Meath had scored a total of 6–44 to Dublin's 3–52 over the four matches.

– Kilkenny no longer have a senior football team, but they won three titles in 1888, 1900 and 1911.

– Dublin have won over twice as many titles (53) as nearest challengers Meath (21).

– Between 1975 and 1978 Leinster champions Dublin

reached four All-Ireland football and National League finals.

– Westmeath won their first and only Leinster Championship in 2004 when they were managed by the late Kerry great Páidí Ó Sé.

Roll of Honour

Dublin (53): 1891, 1892, 1894, 1896, 1897, 1898, 1899, 1901, 1902, 1904, 1906, 1907, 1908, 1920, 1921, 1922, 1923, 1924, 1932, 1933, 1934, 1941, 1942, 1955, 1958, 1959, 1962, 1963, 1965, 1974, 1975, 1976, 1977, 1978, 1979, 1983, 1984, 1985, 1989, 1992, 1993, 1994, 1995, 2002, 2005, 2006, 2007, 2008, 2009, 2011, 2012, 2013, 2014

Meath (21): 1895, 1939, 1940, 1947, 1949, 1951, 1952, 1954, 1964, 1966, 1967, 1970, 1986, 1987, 1988, 1990, 1991, 1996, 1999, 2001, 2010

Kildare (13): 1903, 1905, 1919, 1926, 1927, 1928, 1929, 1930, 1931, 1935, 1956, 1998, 2000

Offaly (10): 1960, 1961, 1969, 1971, 1972, 1973, 1980, 1981, 1982, 1997

Wexford (10): 1890, 1893, 1913, 1914, 1915, 1916, 1917, 1918, 1925, 1945

Louth (8): 1909, 1910, 1912, 1943, 1948, 1950, 1953, 1957

Laois (6): 1889, 1936, 1937, 1938, 1946, 2003

Kilkenny (3): 1888, 1900, 1911

Carlow (1): 1944

Longford (1): 1968

Westmeath (1): 2004

CONNACHT SENIOR FOOTBALL CHAMPIONSHIP

– London and New York both compete in this championship. London reached their first and only decider in 2013.

– Galway were declared winners of the first championship. Mayo were the winners in the first contested final in 1901, defeating Galway.

– Galway represented the province in the All-Ireland series in the early years of the championship. They were declared champions of Connacht, due to unfinished or uncontested championships.

– Mayo won four finals in a row from 1907–10, defeating Galway in two and Roscommon in two. They equalled this achievement in 2014, defeating great rivals Galway in the 2014 final.

– Roscommon won four titles in a row from 1977–80. They defeated Galway in 1977 and 1978, and Mayo in 1979 and 1980.

– Galway went one better with a magnificent five in a row from 1956–60. They defeated Leitrim in 1960 final.

– Galway's All-Ireland win in 1998 ended a Connacht famine that had lasted thirty-two years.

– Leitrim set an unenviable record when losing four finals in a row, from 1957–60. Galway defeated them on all four occasions.

- Mayo may have only won forty-five titles, despite the records showing them at forty-six. One win remains disputed, that of 1939 – the final was never finished but Mayo were awarded the title.

- Mayo and Galway, one of football's great rivalries, was celebrated in the 1998 *Saw Doctors* hit, 'Will Galway beat Mayo?'

- Leitrim scored a famous win in the 1994 decider against red-hot favourites Mayo.

Roll of Honour

Mayo (46): 1901, 1903, 1904, 1906, 1907, 1908, 1909, 1910, 1915, 1916, 1918, 1920, 1921, 1923, 1924, 1929, 1930, 1931, 1932, 1935, 1936, 1937, 1939, 1948, 1949, 1950, 1951, 1955, 1967, 1969, 1981, 1985, 1988, 1989, 1992, 1993, 1996, 1997, 1999, 2004, 2006, 2009, 2011, 2012, 2013, 2014

Galway (44): 1900, 1902, 1911, 1913, 1917, 1919, 1922, 1925, 1926, 1933, 1934, 1938, 1940, 1941, 1942, 1945, 1954, 1956, 1957, 1958, 1959, 1960, 1963, 1964, 1965, 1966, 1968, 1970, 1971, 1973, 1974, 1976, 1982, 1983, 1984, 1986, 1987, 1995, 1998, 2000, 2002, 2003, 2005, 2008

Roscommon (20): 1905, 1912, 1914, 1943, 1944, 1946, 1947, 1952, 1953, 1961, 1962, 1972, 1977, 1978, 1979, 1980, 1990, 1991, 2001, 2010

Sligo (3): 1928, 1975, 2007

Leitrim (2): 1927, 1994

ULSTER SENIOR FOOTBALL CHAMPIONSHIP

- Tyrone has the largest number of football clubs in Ulster (48).

- Fermanagh remain the only Ulster team not to have won an Ulster title.

- Oisín McConville of Armagh became the Ulster Championship's highest scorer in 2007. He surpassed Peter Canavan's (Tyrone) record of 218 points.

- From 2004 until 2006 the final was staged at Croke Park in Dublin.

- St Tiernach's Park in Monaghan has become the spiritual home of the Ulster Football final. It hosted its first final in 1906. It was not the 1906 final however, but the 1904 decider which was being played. Cavan claimed the title defeating Armagh.

- Four out of the last five All-Ireland-winning Ulster sides have crashed out of the provincial championship in the first round. Donegal bucked that trend in 2013 and went on to reach the provincial final before losing out to Monaghan.

- Since 1990 Ulster has provided more All-Ireland winners than any other province.

- RTÉ pundit Joe Brolly was top scorer in the Ulster Championship in 1997. He scored a total of 3–15.

- Donegal have won back-to-back Ulster titles from

the preliminary round (a feat achieved by no other county).

Roll of Honour*

Cavan (39): 1891, 1903, 1904, 1905, 1906, 1915, 1918, 1919, 1920, 1923, 1924, 1925, 1926, 1928, 1931, 1932, 1933, 1934, 1935, 1936, 1937, 1939, 1940, 1941, 1942, 1943, 1944, 1945, 1947, 1948, 1949, 1952, 1954, 1955, 1962, 1964, 1967, 1969, 1997

Monaghan (14): 1888, 1914, 1916, 1917, 1921, 1922, 1927, 1929, 1930, 1938, 1979, 1985, 1988, 2013

Armagh (14): 1890, 1902, 1950, 1953, 1977, 1980, 1982, 1999, 2000, 2002, 2004, 2005, 2006, 2008

Tyrone (13): 1956, 1957, 1973, 1984, 1986, 1989, 1995, 1996, 2001, 2003, 2007, 2009, 2010

Down (12): 1959, 1960, 1961, 1963, 1965, 1966, 1968, 1971, 1978, 1981, 1991, 1994

Antrim (9): 1901, 1908, 1909, 1910, 1911, 1912, 1913, 1946, 1951

Donegal (8): 1972, 1974, 1983, 1990, 1992, 2011, 2012, 2014

Derry (7): 1958, 1970, 1975, 1976, 1987, 1993, 1998

* not contested in 1889, 1892–1900 and 1907

NUMBER 13 AND OTHER AMAZING FACTS

HURLING KINGDOM

Kerry contested their first All-Ireland hurling decider, against Wexford (Crossabeg), in 1891. Ballyduff, the Kerry standard bearers, had been busy in the 'Transfer Market' in the weeks coming up to the decider. Eight of their players were from the Kilmoyley club, which had rather obligingly disbanded, allowing them to sign for Ballyduff. The game ended in high drama, as Crossabeg scored a controversial equalising goal to force extra time. The enraged Ballyduff players claimed the shot had rebounded off a spectator and back into the net. However, the referee turned a deaf ear to their pleas and extra time was required to separate the protagonists.

An incident-packed final period ended in a melee, with the Ballyduff boys clinging on grimly for a two-point victory. It would turn out to be Kerry's only All-Ireland hurling triumph. It would also be the only time they would grace hurling's biggest stage, giving them a 100 per cent winning record. Wearing grey jumpers with a gold band and long trousers, they certainly qualified as the best-dressed champions of all time!

BLUE AND SAFFRON REBELS

The county colours of Cork are among the most recognisable in Gaelic games. It would be hard to imagine

'The Rebels' entering the battlefield without their beloved red and white, but it has happened. Before 1918 Cork wore blue and saffron. After a raid by the British security forces on the Cork County Board offices, their jerseys were stolen. They had to borrow a set of gear from the Fr O'Leary Hall Club until a set of replacements could be purchased. The new kit comprised red jerseys and assorted shorts, and appeared to have an energising effect on The Rebel's fortunes. They ended a sixteen-year famine and won the All-Ireland final. Jimmy Kennedy was on fire and scored four goals as they downed Dublin in the 1919 showpiece. This welcome change in the county's fortunes assured the new jerseys a permanent place in Cork GAA history.

RADIO DAYS

Bill Doonan from Cavan joined the British Army in 1943. He served as a radio operator with an army unit in southern Italy, and brought a whole new meaning to the term 'Missing in Action'.

One Sunday in early September of that year he vanished mysteriously after lunch. The alarm was raised amid rising fears that something untoward had happened. The radio operator was finally located perched in a tree, in a state of deep concentration, with the radio held up to his ear. It transpired that, after much effort, Private Doonan had tuned in to the commentary of the second half of the All-Ireland final between Roscommon and Cavan in Croke Park. Luckily for the proud son of Cavan his superiors did not deem this a court-martialling offence.

The former radio operator would later line out with his beloved Cavan in two All-Ireland football deciders. The first was in the Polo Grounds, New York, in 1947, which, rather ironically, was one of the most famous radio broadcasts of all time.

TAKING HIS POINT

One of the most bizarre moments in GAA history occurred in the 1909 All-Ireland hurling final. With time running out, Kilkenny's Jack Rochford scored a point for Tipperary! The men from the Marble City were hanging on as Tipperary came in search of a much-needed green flag. Multiple All-Ireland winner Rochford gathered the ball close to his own goal, but with half of the Tipperary team bearing down on him, he was in a very perilous position. Fearing a hook or a block down would lead to a goal, he was left with only one option. He elected to scoop the ball over his own bar, much to the chagrin of the great Tom Semple and his 'Premier' crew. It turned out to be as good as a score for the Kilkenny men. The resulting puck out heralded a shrill blast of the referee's whistle calling time on the game. Rochford's quick thinking had ensured victory for the 'Cats' and Tipperary tasted defeat for the first time in an All-Ireland final.

NUMBER 13

No team captained by a player wearing the number thirteen jersey has ever lifted the Sam Maguire Cup since its inception in 1928.

Colm 'Gooch' Cooper of Kerry was the latest victim of the demon digits. With seven minutes to go in the 2011 Senior Football final, the Kingdom were ahead by four points. However, Dublin clawed them back, courtesy of a Kevin McManamon goal and a Kevin Nolan point. Goalkeeper Stephen Cluxton's late heroics then sealed the 'Dub's' great escape.

The number thirteen is the least popular jersey, worn by All-Ireland football final captains. It has only been worn three times on All-Ireland final day: by Colm O'Rourke (Meath) in 1990; Philip Clifford (Cork) in 1999; and Colm Cooper (Kerry) in 2011.

The curse of thirteen does not extend to hurling, however. Three men have lifted the Liam MacCarthy Cup wearing number thirteen: D. J. Carey (Kilkenny) in 2003, Thomas Mulcahy (Cork) in 1990 and Charlie McCarthy (Cork) in 1978. Five players have tasted defeat wearing the number, including Tipperary men Eoin Kelly in 2011 and Nicky English in 1988.

The luckiest number for a captain in football is number eleven, with a whopping sixteen winners. In hurling it is number twelve, which has seen the winners' enclosure on thirteen occasions.

HOME FINAL

Prior to the purchase of Croke Park in 1913, All-Ireland senior finals and semi-finals were played at various locations around the country, such as the Phoenix Park in Dublin and Ballybrit Race Course – not places you would readily associate with the All-Ireland series.

Without doubt the 1904 All-Ireland hurling final was staged in one of the most unique surroundings of them all. Kilkenny and Cork made the journey to Carrick-on-Suir, Tipperary, for an eagerly awaited contest. The venue? GAA ex-President Maurice Davin's farm! The teams served up a thrilling contest, with the result in the balance right up to the very end. Pat 'Fox' Maher, the Kilkenny custodian, made a wonder save to deny the last throw of the Cork dice. The 'Cats' prevailed on a 1–9 to 1–8 scoreline. It was their first All-Ireland victory, secured in the heart of Tipperary!

THE DRIVE FOR FIVE

Despite many near misses, no senior inter-county side has ever won five All-Ireland championships in a row. Kilkenny were the latest victims as bitter rivals Tipperary ended their 'drive for five' in 2010 in a deluge of goals.

Cork are the only other hurling team to win four titles. Captained by Seán Condon they defeated Dublin in the 1944 decider, but came unstuck the following year at the Thurles Sports Field, as Tipperary prevailed on a 2–13 to 3–2 scoreline.

Wexford footballers and Kerry (twice) have also perished at the gates of All-Ireland immortality. The Kingdom came closest to the Holy Grail in 1982. Entering the final minutes of the competition, the concession of a free by Eoin Liston would prove very costly. Eugene McGee, the Offaly manager, had introduced a sub as the final entered its dying embers. While many may have missed the arrival of Seamus Darby, he would have an impact that would resonate through GAA history. Darby out-fielded Kerry's Tommy Doyle and smashed the ball past a stunned Charlie Nelligan. Legend indicates that this was the final play of the match, but there was still time for the Kingdom to respond. Tom Spillane had a final shot which dropped short and Offaly held on to break Kerry hearts.

PUKE FOOTBALL

Guinness Brewery side Young Ireland's can lay claim to be the first side that employed 'the Blanket Defence'. In the 1891 All-Ireland senior football final, with Cork champions Clondrohid chasing a goal, the Dublin representatives resorted to tactics that would not be out of place in the modern game. With a goal out-weighing any number of points, Young Ireland's protected their net with the motto 'Thou shalt not pass'. They massed all twenty-one players in front of their own goal, a tactic that would eventually bear fruit. While Clondrohid did score two goals and were awarded the match on the field of play, there was a twist in the saga. The referee, after much deliberation (three hours), decided that a Cork player had picked the ball off the ground in the act of scoring. The Dublin team were granted a replay, but Clondrohid refused to travel. By the time of the next replay Clondrohid had disbanded, and so the inventors of 'the Blanket' took the All-Ireland title.

HAVING A BALL

The 1890 Munster Senior Football final was between fierce Munster rivals, Cork and Kerry. They would have many exciting duels in the following years, but this final was destined to end without a winner. The Munster showpiece has known many a dramatic ending, but none quite like this. With just three minutes remaining on the clock, the ball burst and despite frantic efforts to find a replacement, none could be located. The onus was on Kilorglin of Kerry, who had been nominated to provide a spare ball. Sadly they had forgotten to bring one.

It was a brief stay of execution, however, as the Cork standard bearers (Midleton) prevailed in the replay.

THE UNFORGETTABLE JOURNEY

When Mick O'Connell captained Kerry to glory in the 1959 All-Ireland football final, it was the start of an incredible journey ... back home!

The reclusive Kerry great was never a man to stand on ceremony, and he made a quick exit after the match. He left the cheering crowds behind him and the Sam Maguire in the safe hands of his comrades. Boarding a train, he made tracks home to the Kingdom. The proud son of Valentia then departed the mainland in his customary mode of transport. Stepping into his trusty currach, he picked up the oars and set sail for the island! Soon he was but a shadow in the gathering gloom.

He would make that journey many times, from the heaving sea of faces in Croke Park to the tranquil shores of home. The gentle giant from Valentia would go on to win another three All-Ireland medals before he rowed into Gaelic football immortality.

MATT GIVES DUBLIN THE BOOT

Matt Gallagher of Donegal lined out at full-back in the 1992 All-Ireland senior football final. Their opponents were Dublin and a busy afternoon was expected for the Donegal back. Clare had provided the shock of the championship by downing the mighty Kerry in Munster, but the 'Dubs' had ended the fairytale and were hot favourites to dispatch the Tir Conaill men.

Donegal had not read the script, however, and went on to win on a 0–18 to 0–14 scoreline. During the game Matt Gallagher went on to set a very unusual record. He never kicked the ball once in the entire game!

THE DUBLIN ALL-STARS

Dublin beat Cork by 0–5 to 0–4 in the 1906 All-Ireland football final. The low-scoring match was played in Athy, County Kildare. The same two teams played out a similar low-scoring match the following year, as Dublin edged it again, 0–6 to 0–2.

The winning Dublin teams certainly had an All-Ireland look about them. They were made up of players from ten different counties. Within their ranks were players from all corners of Ireland. There was, however, one noticeable absentee. Not one of them was from the capital city!

THE MAN IN THE CAP

Peter McDermott holds a unique slot in GAA folklore. The Navan O'Mahony's clubman is the only man to have refereed an All-Ireland final before and after winning one.

In 1953 he refereed the All-Ireland football final between Kerry and Armagh. The following year he would return to Croke Park, this time as a player, lining out for his native Meath against most of the Kerry team he had refereed the previous year. McDermott would go on to claim a winners' medal as the 'Royals' defeated the Kingdom by six points. In 1956 he took charge of the final between Cork and Galway.

His playing exploits also consisted of five All-Ireland final appearances in four years (including a replay). He truly was a man of many parts: he had a stint as secretary of the Meath county board and was also a member of the coaching staff when Meath won another All-Ireland in 1967. He was also jointly credited, along with Harry Beitzel of Australia, with starting the International Compromise Rules Series. McDermott collaborated with Beitzel to arrange a two-match tour by an Australian Rules side to Ireland. The Australians played and defeated reigning All-Ireland champions Meath at Croke Park in October 1967 under Gaelic football rules. When the International series started formally in 1984, he was manager of the Irish team.

DOUBLE VISION

One of the highlights of the 'Clare breakthrough years' was their 1997 Munster Hurling final defeat of bitter foes Tipperary. Ger Loughnane would later acclaim it as one of the sweetest victories ever.

They say lightning never strikes twice, but sadly for Tipperary's ace forward John Leahy it did in that fateful season. In a sweltering Páirc Uí Chaoimh on 6 July 'The Banner' finally put one over on the 'Premier' county, on Munster's biggest stage. In the final moments of the decider, with the Clare men ahead by a goal, the ball broke to the unmarked Tipperary talisman Leahy. As he prepared to hit the bouncing ball, Clare supporters, of whom 43,000 were attending, offered up thousands of silent Novenas. But the ball hit a divot and Leahy scuffed his shot.

Clare had finally beaten Tipperary in a Munster decider and amazingly lightning would strike again later that year. Tipperary availed of the new back-door system and made it through to face their Munster conquerors again. In yet another close encounter of the Munster kind, 'The Banner' were ahead by a slender point when Leahy got the opportunity to exorcise his demons. Ignoring the pleas of his supporters to take an equalising point, the Mullinahone man went for a goal. He got a good connection, but Clare goalie Davy Fitzgerald was equal to the task and batted the ball away. Moments later, when Conor Gleeson's shot drifted wide, it was all over and Clare had an unlikely double against their great Munster rivals and long-time tormentors.

THOU SHALT NOT PLAY HURLING

In the fourteenth century, Kilkenny, kings of the modern game, attempted to ban hurling. This occurred in 1367 when the infamous Statutes of Kilkenny threatened to fine and imprison anyone found playing the game. The fine print of the stark message declared 'do not, henceforth, use the plays which men call horlings, with great sticks and a ball upon the ground, from which great evils and maims have arisen'. However, the law was largely ignored on the banks of the Nore. The game eventually prospered and the 'Cats' bared their claws. They are now such a dominant force in inter-county hurling that the possibility exists that the law may be revisited at the next GAA Congress!

MAN OF THE MATCH

In the 2010 Senior Hurling final Lar Corbett won the Man of the Match award after halting Kilkenny's bid for an unprecedented five-in-a-row.

Corbett was a late developer and did not feature at minor level for Tipperary. His career really blossomed under the stewardship of Liam Sheedy, who handed him a licence to roam around the forward line. Blessed with lightning pace and a keen eye for goal, the Thurles Sarsfields clubman was seen at his very best in the 2010 final against Kilkenny.

Tipperary had come close a year previously against 'The Cats', and Corbett and his team-mates were on a revenge mission against their arch rivals. The man from

Thurles was on fire and everything he touched turned to gold. Corbett seemed to be everywhere, but while his input to the outcome of the game was immense, he actually had fewer touches than nearly all the other players on the field. With just seven touches, however, he amassed a staggering return of three goals. This remarkable haul led to Lar being named RTÉ Man of the Match and he was also named 'Hurler of the Year'.

YOUNG AT HEART

Who is the oldest inter-county player? With the average age of a GAA player becoming younger with each passing season, players in their late thirties are now a dying breed.

Leitrim is a county better known for its football than its hurling, yet the hurlers are an integral part of the Lory Meagher Cup for fourth tier teams. They can lay claim to having had one of the oldest players at inter-county level. The man in question is Tommy McLoughlin, the Leitrim goalkeeper who lined out in the 2012 Lory Meagher Cup aged forty-seven! Tommy made his debut for his beloved county in 1985 and togged out for his club in 2014.

Tommy is still, however, just a 'young fella' compared to some of the more senior members of the GAA family. St Gabriel's of London went into battle in 2013 with a new corner-forward. Kerril Burke proved a match winner when striking late in the Division 2 London fixture. Burke, who doubles up as club chairman, netted the winner at the tender age of seventy-four!

AGE-OLD FOOTBALL RIVALRY

When you think of Kilkenny and Tipperary, one of hurling's ancient rivalries springs to mind. Yet when teams from the two counties met in the 1900 All-Ireland semi-final, there wasn't a hurley in sight.

On that occasion they traded blows with the bigger ball and, in the finest traditions of these two Gaelic giants, the game didn't lack drama. Slate Quarries, the Leinster Champions from Kilkenny, won the match and advanced to the All-Ireland final. The victory did not go down well with the men from the Premier county, who lodged an objection. It emerged that five of the Kilkenny team (which was largely comprised of quarry workers) were from Tipperary and not eligible to represent the Leinster Kingpins. Tipperary were duly awarded the match, defeating London in the final. The winning Tipperary team was backboned by the 'Famous Five' quarrymen, who had originally lined out with Kilkenny!

THE BANNER SLAYS THE KINGDOM

19 July 1992 – this has become known as the day of the 'Munster Football Miracle', yet no title can do justice to the events that happened on that unforgettable day in the Limerick Gaelic Grounds.

Clare's only provincial football title for ninety-five years represented one of the great shocks of the modern era. Along with Tipperary, who won in 1935, they are the only team to have broken the Kerry/Cork monopoly on the Munster Senior Football trophy.

At the end of 1991 an open draw system replaced the usual seeded championship in Munster. It offered the underdogs a chance to gain a rare berth in the Munster Senior decider. The Clare men made good use of this opportunity, dispatching Tipperary in the semi-final.

For the final 25,000 souls packed into the Limerick Gaelic Grounds, more in hope than expectation, for the novel pairing of the Kingdom versus 'The Banner'. The Clare men tore into their more illustrious opponents from the off, but a lack of composure cost them dearly. An early penalty was missed by Gerry Killeen and some wild shooting made an upset seem highly improbable.

However, Kerry seemed to be lacking their normal fluidity and found scores hard to come by, with only the mercurial Maurice Fitzgerald keeping them in touch from placed balls.

The defining moment of the game came when Colm Clancy blasted the ball into the Kerry net. When James Hanrahan made a wonder save against Kerry talisman Fitzgerald, the writing was on the wall for Mickey 'Ned' O'Sullivan's charges. Despite Kerry driving hard late on, a great catch and solo run from Tom Morrissey set up Gerry Killeen for the clinching score.

When Francis McInerney, the Clare captain, was handed the ball at the end by referee Paddy Russell, there were a few seconds of confusion before he blew the final whistle. Clare had beaten Kerry for the first time in sixty years.

THEY DIED WITH THEIR BOOTS OFF

The old Western movie adage of 'They died with their boots on' certainly did not apply to the 1889 All-Ireland hurling final.

Tulla, representing Clare, took to the field, to the astonishment of their Dublin opponents, minus a very important part of their playing gear. Despite the fact the underfoot conditions were slippery, they had elected to play without football boots!

The barefooted wonders started well and were in front at the break (1–5 to 1–0). Their opponents, Kickhams, were badly in need of some inspiration and W. J. Spain was the man to provide it. He hit three quick-fire goals to take Dublin into a lead they never lost.

Sadly for the Clare standard bearers their bold gamble had backfired and they were left nursing more than sore feet! Dublin won their first All-Ireland on a 5–1 to 1–6 scoreline.

MOVING THE GOALPOSTS

The sixth All-Ireland hurling final provided plenty of drama before the ball was even thrown in. When they arrived for the final the Cork and Kilkenny teams refused to play on the Ashtown pitch. The reason? Someone had neglected to mow the grass!

It seemed the first ever championship meeting between the 'Rebels' and the 'Cats' would end before it even started. Disaster was averted, however, as they reached a compromise on the venue. It was agreed to play the final in a different location nearby. The players carried the goalposts to the Phoenix Park and played the final there!

Cork, represented by famous club side Blackrock, romped to a 6–8 to 0–2 win.

JOHN 3:7

When Brian Carthy of RTÉ uttered the immortal lines – 'A wonder score by Joe Canning. That young man can walk on water. From now on it should be Joe 4:7 instead of John 3:7.' – not only was the popular commentator paying homage to one of the modern games' greatest players, he was also paying homage to one of its greatest fans.

Regular GAA fans have often seen a banner, bearing the now familiar message John 3:7. It is a common sight at GAA grounds around the country. The bright yellow banner has now been an integral part of the Irish sporting summer for over two decades. But who is behind the famous biblical banner and what does it mean?

The man who carries the banner is not named John. Rather his name is Frank Hogan. Formerly a Tipperary native, he now lives in County Limerick. The banner reads: 'Marvel not that I said unto thee, You must be born again.' It is part of verse 3:7 from the Gospel of John. Frank is a born-again Christian. The message reminds us that we must repent our sins in order to be born again. Frank is an avid GAA fan and where better to display the banner than in his other place of worship!

A MATTER OF TIME

Brendan Lynch was born in the shadow of Ireland's highest mountain, Carrantuohill in Kerry. Brendan played for the Beaufort club in the Kingdom and also had a very successful footballing brother named Paudie. The Kerry man certainly knows a thing or two about time! He lined out in six All-Ireland finals and won three All-Ireland medals with a difference. Over the years the playing time of hurling and football matches has been increased from 60 to 80 minutes, and then reduced to 70 minutes. He is the only Gaelic footballer to have won All-Ireland medals in a 60-, 70- and 80-minute final.

THE THUNDER AND LIGHTNING FINAL

The 1939 All-Ireland hurling final between Cork and Kilkenny was played in a furious thunder storm. Dubbed 'the Thunder and Lightning final', the game matched the elements, as both teams hurled up a Croke Park classic.

While Ireland had declared its neutrality on the outbreak of war, there was a nervous feel to All-Ireland final day, 3 September. Torrential rain began to fall, as the grave news of impending conflict broke. The heavy rain meant a lot of fans could not travel, and many chose to gather around the comfort of their firesides and listen to the radio instead.

A final ultimatum had been given to Adolf Hitler by Britain and France. The German dictator chose to ignore the warning, and a declaration of war was now inevitable. At 11.27 a.m. in London, air sirens signalled that the world was at war. Despite the bad tidings and inclement weather, almost 40,000 hardy souls made the pilgrimage to hurling headquarters for the match.

Cork and Kilkenny turned on the style against a backdrop of heavy rain, thunder and lightning. Cork started with the wind at their backs, but contrived to be six points in arrears at the break.

However, as the storm broke early in the second half, the 'Rebels' staged an amazing fightback, aided by a barnstorming performance from future Taoiseach Jack Lynch.

As the clock ticked into injury time the sides were level, but despite the men from Leeside's stirring effort, the 'Cats' had the final say. Jimmy Kelly lofted over the winning score to break Cork hearts.

THE FIRST ALL-IRELAND

The first All-Ireland hurling final holds a unique record all of its own. Tipperary (Thurles) defeated Galway (Mellick) 1–1 to 0–0. It is recorded in the Guinness Book of Records as the lowest scoring hurling match of all time.

The match took place in Hoare's field in Birr, County Offaly, before an estimated attendance of 5,000 people. The site is today marked by a monument that is situated close to the new Tesco store.

The match was played on Sunday 1 April 1887, with the players togging out at a nearby hotel. The pitch was slightly bigger than the fields of today and each team had twenty-one players instead of fifteen, leading to a very congested playing area. This probably contributed to the paltry total of scores.

There was also a different scoring system in place. A goal out-scored any amount of points. There were also forfeit points awarded. Forfeit points were awarded in place of 65s. Five forfeit points equalled one real point, but these were only used in the event of a draw.

In any event the pocket calculators were not required, as the Tipperary men, captained by Jim Stapleton, prevailed by the minimum goals and points total. Galway also had an unnamed player sent off and, in an act of outstanding sportsmanship, withdrew a player to tend to an injured Tipperary man who had fallen on his hurley.

TAILOR-MADE SUCCESS

As with all games of such magnitude, many a player has attested to having a sleepless night before the 'Big One'. However, Dunmanway (Cork), who contested the 1897 Senior Football final with Kickhams (Dublin), brought this to a whole new level.

Arriving at 2 a.m. in the capital, they were alarmed to discover that no one had bothered to book them a hotel. They were left with little option but to trek around the city on foot in search of somewhere to 'Pitch their Tent'! A weary Dunmanway squad eventually gained admittance into a hotel in Amiens Street and succumbed to some badly needed sleep.

Their ordeal continued on the pitch the next day, as 'The Dubs' poured on the agony. The Cork men had no answer to William Guiry's two goals and lost by ten points.

You could say this Dublin side was 'tailor-made' for success. It was made up of drapers: seven who worked in Cleary's, four in Arnott's and others from Todd's and the Henry Street Warehouse.

WEXFORD SLAY THE THREE KINGS

The National Hurling League final of 1956 was contested by Wexford and Tipperary. By half-time Wexford were trailing Tipperary by fifteen points. However, within minutes of the re-start Nicky Rackard had launched an amazing comeback.

Rackard was in inspired form and, despite the attentions of two defenders, he palmed the ball past a bemused Tony Reddin in the Tipperary goal. He then set up three further goals to put the Wexford men a point clear. Rackard added another goal in the closing minutes of the game, and Wexford had risen from their graves.

The reigning All-Ireland champions had fashioned hurling's version of the 'Great Escape'. The final score after a titanic battle was Wexford 5–9 to Tipperary's 2–14.

Now en route to a second All-Ireland final in a row, they defeated Kilkenny in the Leinster final by a solitary point: 4–8 to 3–10. The All-Ireland final would be a repeat of the 1954 decider against Cork, when the Leesiders prevailed. On that day 'The Wizard of Cloyne', Christy Ring, was going for a record-breaking eighth Celtic Cross. Such was the interest in the game that the gates were shut thirty-five minutes before the throw-in. It seemed the entire county of Wexford had descended en masse to the capital. Every man, woman and child, and even the odd dog, appeared to have made the pilgrimage!

In front of an attendance of 84,856 expectant souls, Wexford hearts were broken. Ring had a haul of five points and a shout for a goal, which was given as a seventy instead. A ball had struck Wexford's full-back Nick O'Donnell with such force that it broke his collarbone. The Rebels were 1–9 to 1–6 winners and claimed a third All-Ireland in a row.

The 1956 decider offered the 'Yellow bellies' the opportunity to exact swift revenge. Owing to an outbreak of polio in Cork, the final was delayed by a number of weeks. When it did get underway, Wexford made the perfect start. Tim Flood, a lifelong musician, hit the perfect note with the opening point. Podge Kehoe then gave them just the tonic they needed, with his goal leaving them four clear when many of the patrons had barely taken their seats.

It was 1–6 to 0–5 at the break, and Wexford forged seven clear with a Martin Codd solo run followed by a delightful point. The game now was running away from Cork, but then Christy Ring stood over a close-in free. A hush fell over the crowd. The great man gave the ball a cold stare. He lifted the sliotar and sent a rocket to the back of the net.

The two magnificent teams continued to trade blows. Terry Kelly sent Cork on the attack and Paddy Barry goaled past Art Foley to put his team in the ascendancy.

Nicky Rackard steadied the Wexford ship with a point and then added two more from frees.

Then, a moment came that turned Wexford blood cold. Ring was bearing down on goal and all Wexford eyes in the crowd were shut, as hurried prayers were uttered. When they re-opened the unthinkable had happened – the ball had been saved by Foley.

With Ring denied, the purple and gold were re-energised. Nicky Rackard shrugged off the attentions of his marker to get on the end of a Tom Ryan hand-pass. The Rebels were reeling now and Rackard applied the knock-out blow. He lowered his shoulders and hit a rasper past Mick Cashman in the Cork goal. The Slaneysiders were now five points to the good, 2–13 to 2–8. Tom Dixon embellished the scoreboard with a quick-fire point. At the final whistle Ring was carried shoulder high by Bobby Rackard and Nick O'Donnell in an act of sportsmanship that typified the camaraderie and respect of a wonderful sporting contest.

Confucius once said, 'The journey of a thousand miles begins with the first step.' It can't be reliably ascertained if the great Chinese philosopher gained entry to the Wexford dressing room during the interval of the National League final. One thing was for sure: Wexford's long march from a fifteen-point deficit in that dramatic encounter to All-Ireland glory in September was one of the ancient game's greatest journeys. They had overcome the 'Three Kings' of hurling – Tipperary, Kilkenny and Cork – in one unforgettable season.

There would be no ninth All-Ireland medal for the great Christy Ring. He would never win another.

ALL-IRELAND CLUB CHAMPIONSHIP

FOOTBALL

- The first winners in the 1970–71 season were an East Kerry divisional team.

- St Finbarr's of Cork are the only team to win both the hurling and football club titles. 'The Barrs' completed the double with a win over Ballinasloe in 1980.

- The Andy Merrigan Cup was first awarded in 1974, donated by the Castletown club in memory of the great Wexford footballer who died in a farming accident at the height of his career.

- Dublin clubs (UCD (2) and St Vincent's of Raheny) won three All-Irelands in a row from 1974–76.

- Limerick's Thomond College took the All-Ireland crown in 1978. They had within their ranks Kerry great Pat Spillane, but not one player was from Limerick.

- Kerry and Cork clubs took a stranglehold on the competition, winning nine titles in thirteen years from 1977–89, including four for the famed Cork club Nemo Rangers.

- Clan na nGael (Drum and Clonown) won seven Connacht titles in eight years (1983–90), but did not win a single All-Ireland.

- Burren of Down ended a fourteen-year Ulster drought when they were victorious in 1986.

- Baltinglass caused a major shock in 1990 by winning the first national honour for them and Wicklow.

- Six-time winners Crossmaglen Rangers have been Ulster champions ten times and Armagh champions forty times.

- Twenty-six different clubs have won the championship.

- Amalgamations of clubs are no longer allowed to enter the All-Ireland Club Championship.

Roll of Honour

Nemo Rangers (Cork) (7): 1973, 1979, 1982, 1984, 1989, 1994, 2003

Crossmaglen Rangers (Armagh) (6): 1997, 1999, 2000, 2007, 2011, 2012

St Finbarr's (Cork) (3): 1980, 1981, 1987

St Vincent's (Dublin) (3): 1976, 2008, 2014

UCD (Dublin) (2): 1974, 1975

Burren (Down) (2): 1986, 1988

Kilmacud Crokes (Dublin) (2): 1995, 2009

East Kerry (1): 1971

Bellaghy (Derry) (1): 1972

Austin Stacks (Kerry) (1): 1977

Thomond College (Limerick) (1): 1978

Portlaoise (Laois) (1): 1983

Castleisland Desmonds (Kerry) (1): 1985

Baltinglass (Wicklow) (1): 1990

Lavey (Derry) (1): 1991

Dr Crokes (Kerry) (1): 1992

O'Donovan Rossa (Cork) (1): 1993

Laune Rangers (Kerry) (1): 1996

Corofin (Galway) (1): 1998

Crossmolina (Mayo) (1): 2001

Ballinderry (Derry) (1): 2002

Caltra (Galway) (1): 2004

Ballina Stephenites (Mayo) (1): 2005

Salthill-Knocknacarra (Galway) (1): 2006

St Gall's (Antrim) (1): 2010

St Brigid's (Roscommon) (1): 2013

ALL-IRELAND CLUB SENIOR HURLING CHAMPIONSHIP

- The club championship was first held in 1970–71, with Roscrea of Tipperary becoming the first champions.

- Including Portumna (2014), Galway teams have won six of the last nine championships.

- James Stephens of Kilkenny were the first Leinster team to win the competition.

- Castlegar won Connacht's first title in 1980.

- The 1980 final saw Castlegar of Galway go into battle with five Connolly brothers. Their opponents, Ballycastle from Antrim, had no less than six Donnelly brothers in their team.

- In 1983 Loughgiel Shamrocks became Ulster's first All-Ireland champions, repeating the feat in 2012.

- In defeating De La Salle of Waterford in the 2009 final, Portumna of Galway won a third title in four years, the first club to manage this feat.

- Cork teams reached eight of the first nine finals, winning seven of them.

- Ballyhale Shamrocks have won the most All-Ireland Club titles, with five wins.

- Birr and Portumna have four wins each.

Finals and Winners

2013–14: Portumna, Galway

2012–13: St Thomas's, Galway

2011–12: Loughgiel, Antrim

2010–11: Clarinbridge, Galway

2009–10: Ballyhale Shamrocks, Kilkenny

2008–09: Portumna, Galway

2007–08: Portumna, Galway

2006–07: Ballyhale Shamrocks, Kilkenny

2005–06: Portumna, Galway

2004–05: James Stephens, Kilkenny

2003–04: Newtownshandrum, Cork

2002–03: Birr, Offaly

2001–02: Birr, Offaly

2000–01: Athenry, Galway

1999–00: Athenry, Galway

1998–99: St Joseph's, Clare

1997–98: Birr, Offaly

1996–97: Athenry, Galway

1995–96: Sixmilebridge, Clare

1994–95: Birr, Offaly

1993–94: Sarsfields, Galway

1992–93: Sarsfields, Galway

1991–92: Kiltormer, Galway

1990–91: Glenmore, Kilkenny

1989–90: Ballyhale Shamrocks, Kilkenny

1988–89: Buffers Alley, Wexford

1987–88: Midleton, Cork

1986–87: Borrisoleigh, Tipperary

1985–86: Kilruane MacDonaghs, Tipperary

1984–85: St Martin's, Kilkenny

1983–84: Ballyhale Shamrocks, Kilkenny

1982–83: Loughgiel, Antrim

1981–82: James Stephens, Kilkenny

1980–81: Ballyhale Shamrocks, Kilkenny

1979–80: Castlegar, Galway

1978–79: Blackrock, Cork

1977–78: St Finbarr's, Cork

1976–77: Glen Rovers, Cork

1975–76: James Stephens, Kilkenny

1974–75: St Finbarr's, Cork

1973–74: Blackrock, Cork

1972–73: Glen Rovers, Cork

1971–72: Blackrock, Cork

1970–71: Roscrea, Tipperary

GAA ON TELEVISION AND RADIO

– The first time that Gaelic games were seen on Irish television was on 17 March 1962, when Telefís Éireann broadcast live coverage of the Railway Cup hurling final between Munster and Leinster.

– The first radio broadcast was in 1926. 2RN carried a live commentary by renowned Gaelic games journalist P. D. Mehigan of Kilkenny's All-Ireland hurling semi-final victory over Galway. It was also the first live radio broadcast of a field game outside of the United States.

– There was a major shock in the 1959 Munster Hurling Championship at the Cork Athletic Grounds. All-Ireland champions Tipperary were trounced by minnows Waterford. Tipperary played against the wind in the opening half and failed to score. Waterford tore into their much vaunted opponents, registering eight goals and two points. When Michael O'Hehir, who was commentating on a match in the Connacht Football Championship, announced the half-time score on radio, he advised listeners that it must be a joke.

– On 5 September 1971 history was made again when Tipperary's defeat of Kilkenny in the All-Ireland final was the first game to be broadcast in colour.

– The first edition of the popular GAA show *The*

Sunday Game was broadcast on RTÉ on Sunday 8 July 1979. It was presented by Galway-based journalist Jim Carney. There was only one match shown: the Munster hurling final between Cork and Limerick.

– During the entire 1980s the only coverage was live showings of the All-Ireland finals and semi-finals in both hurling and football.

– The first ever Munster hurling final screened live was the 1989 match between Tipperary and Waterford in Páirc Uí Chaoimh.

– In 2007 *The Sunday Game* broadcast a total of fifty live championship games, but in 2008 it only broadcast forty. The decreased number was due to the fact that TV3 was granted the rights to show live championship games for the first time ever. Some former presenters of the show include:

> Jim Carney
> Seán Óg Ó Ceallacháin
> Michael Lyster
> Pat Spillane
> Des Cahill (present).

A whole host of former GAA stars have acted in the role of pundits on the show:

Hurling: Jimmy Barry-Murphy, Eddie Brennan, Jimmy Brohan, D. J. Carey, Eamon Cregan, Anthony Daly, John Doyle, Michael Duignan, Cyril Farrell,

Davy Fitzgerald, Paul Flynn, Pete Finnerty, Pat Hartigan, Pat Henderson, Liam Griffin, Thomas Ryan, Eddie Keher, Phil 'Fan' Larkin, Ger Loughnane, Thomas Mulcahy, Larry O'Gorman, Donal O'Grady, Declan Ruth, Liam Sheedy, Donal Óg Cusack.

Football: Kevin Armstrong, Joe Brolly, Martin Carney, Enda Colleran, Paul Curran, Tony Davis, Sean Flanagan, Coman Goggins, Kevin Heffernan, Joe Lennon, Tommy Lyons, Jim McDonnell, Kevin McStay, Mick O'Connell, Mick O'Dwyer, Sean O'Neill, Anthony Tohill, Dave Weldrick, Eamonn Young, Colm O'Rourke, Kieran Whelan, Eamonn O'Hara.

FAMOUS COMMENTATORS

Michael O'Hehir

- He had just turned eighteen and was still attending school when he wrote to Radio Éireann asking to do a test commentary.

- He was given a five-minute microphone test during the opening half of a GAA league match. The director of broadcasting at RTÉ, Dr T. J. Kiernan, was so impressed with O'Hehir's unique style that he allowed him to commentate on the whole of the second half.

- In August 1938 O'Hehir made his first official broadcast – the All-Ireland football semi-final between Monaghan and Galway. He went on to commentate on the second semi-final and that year's final between Galway and Kerry.

- The following year he covered his first hurling final, the 1939 decider between Cork and Kilkenny.

- In 1947 he gave a memorable commentary on the All-Ireland football final from the Polo Grounds in New York city. Over 1,000,000 people were listening to the broadcast back in Ireland. The historic broadcast had to be finished by five o'clock New York time, but the final had started late. The last few minutes of O'Hehir's commentary included him pleading with the RTÉ broadcast technicians not to pull the plug and allow him to stay on air. Thankfully his pleas were successful and an enthralled nation back home were able to listen to the game in full.

- The broadcasting great commentated on ninety-nine All-Irelands. His last was the 1984 decider between Kerry and Dublin. He was due to complete his hundredth in August 1985 when he became ill. He died in 1997.

Mícheál Ó Muircheartaigh

- He was born in Dún Síon just outside Dingle, County Kerry, in 1930.

- His first match was a commentary in Irish on the 1949 Railway Cup final on St Patrick's Day.

- When Michael O'Hehir was forced to retire in the mid-1980s, Ó Muircheartaigh was viewed as his natural successor and took over as RTÉ's leading radio commentator.

- Ó Muircheartaigh's love of radio meant that he rarely featured on television.

- Ó Muircheartaigh's commentaries for RTÉ Radio 1's *Sunday Sport* show won him a Jacob's Award in 1992.

- On 16 September 2010 he announced his retirement from broadcasting.

- The last All-Ireland he commentated on was the 2010 All-Ireland senior football final between Cork and Down.

- The final time he took the microphone was for the second test of the International Rules in 2010.

TOP TWENTY GAA TELEVISION MOMENTS

In 2005 the public were asked to choose their favourites from twenty memorable moments drawn from the last forty years of GAA action. These moments had been selected by ten RTÉ sports personalities. A special programme was broadcast showing the results and included the views of the ten selected judges: Des Cahill, Jim Carney, Ger Canning, Brian Carthy, Michael Lyster, Jimmy Magee, Marty Morrissey, Tony O'Donoghue, Mícheál Ó Muircheartaigh and Darragh Maloney. There were also discussions with former players as to their views regarding the best moments.

The public ranked the top twenty thus:

1   **Michael Donnellan's solo run:** All-Ireland football final, Galway v Kildare. Croke Park, 27 September 1998.

2   **Maurice Fitzgerald's sideline:** All-Ireland football quarter-final, Kerry v Dublin. Croke Park, 4 August 2001.

3   **Seamus Darby's last-minute goal:** All-Ireland football final, Offaly v Kerry. Croke Park, 16 September 1982.

4   **John Fenton's goal:** Munster Hurling semi-final (replay), Cork v Limerick. Semple Stadium, 28 June 1987.

5   **Davy Fitzgerald's penalty goal:** Munster Hurling final, Clare v Limerick. Semple Stadium, 9 July 1995.

6   **Kevin Foley's goal:** Leinster Football Championship first round (third replay), Meath v Dublin. Croke Park, 6 July 1991.

7   **D. J. Carey's point:** All-Ireland hurling final, Kilkenny v Clare. Croke Park, 8 September 2002.

8   **Joe Connolly's victory speech:** All-Ireland hurling final, Galway v Limerick. Croke Park, 7 September 1980.

9   **Jack O'Shea's goal:** All-Ireland Fooball final, Kerry v Offaly. Croke Park, 20 September 1981.

10 **Offaly's comeback:** All-Ireland hurling final, Offaly v Limerick. Croke Park, 4 September 1994.

11 **Mattie McDonagh's goal:** All-Ireland football final, Galway v Meath. Croke Park, 25 September 1966.

12 **Mikey Sheehy's lob over Paddy Cullen:** All-Ireland football final, Kerry v Dublin. Croke Park, 24 September 1978.

13 **Babs Keating's barefoot play:** All-Ireland hurling final, Tipperary v Kilkenny. Croke Park, 5 September 1971.

14 **Peter Canavan's return in the 2003 All-Ireland football final:** Tyrone v Armagh. Croke Park, 28 September 2003.

15 **Jimmy Barry-Murphy's goal:** All-Ireland football final, Cork v Galway. Croke Park, 23 September 1973.

16 **Eddie Keher's first goal:** All-Ireland senior hurling final, Kilkenny v Cork. Croke Park, 3 September 1972.

17 **Paddy Cullen's penalty save:** All-Ireland football final, Dublin v Galway. Croke Park, 22 September 1974.

18 **Barney Rock's goal:** National Football League

quarter-final, Dublin v Cork. Croke Park, 5 April 1987.

19 **Frank McGuigan's point-scoring:** Ulster Football final, Tyrone v Armagh. St Tiernach's Park, 15 July 1984.

20 **Offaly fans' sit-down protest:** All-Ireland hurling semi-final, Offaly v Clare. Croke Park, 22 August 1998.

NATIONAL LEAGUES

HURLING

- The National Hurling League (NHL) was first held in 1925–26, thirty-eight years after the first All-Ireland Senior Hurling Championship. Cork were the first winners.

- The 1956 NHL final saw Wexford complete one of the greatest comebacks in GAA history. Trailing by fifteen points at half-time, they came back to win by four points against Tipperary.

- When Pat Leamy lined out in the 1951 NHL final for New York he was aged fifty-three.

- In 2002 the league was changed to a February–April calendar, which has increased interest, with attendances growing and live games broadcast on TG4.

- The Division One title has been won at least once by ten different counties, nine of which have won the title more than once.

- Kerry caused a sensation when they drew their Division 1B match with fallen giants Kilkenny in 1980.

- The all-time record-holders are Tipperary, who have won the competition nineteen times.

- Cavan are the only county who do not compete in the competition.

- Munster is the most successful province and has provided forty-nine winners of Division 1A. Leinster with twenty-four and Connacht with nine (all Galway) are next.

Roll of Honour*

Tipperary (19): 1928, 1949, 1950, 1952, 1954, 1955, 1957, 1959, 1960, 1961, 1964, 1965, 1968, 1979, 1988, 1994, 1999, 2001, 2008

Kilkenny (17): 1933, 1962, 1966, 1976, 1982, 1983, 1986, 1990, 1995, 2002, 2003, 2005, 2006, 2009, 2012, 2013, 2014

Cork (14): 1926, 1930, 1940, 1941, 1948, 1953, 1969, 1970, 1972, 1974, 1980, 1981, 1993, 1998

Limerick (11): 1934, 1935, 1936, 1937, 1938, 1947, 1971, 1984, 1985, 1992, 1997

Galway (9): 1931, 1951, 1975, 1987, 1989, 1996, 2000, 2004, 2010

Wexford (4): 1956, 1958, 1967, 1973

Dublin (3): 1929, 1939, 2011

Clare (3): 1946, 1977, 1978

Waterford (2): 1963, 2007

Offaly (1): 1991

* not contested in 1927, 1932 and 1942–45

FOOTBALL

- The National Football League was first held in 1925–26, thirty-eight years after the first All-Ireland

Senior Football Championship. Laois won the inaugural league.

- The winning team receives the New Ireland Cup, presented by the New Ireland Assurance Company. It was first presented in 1929.

- When Monaghan beat Armagh in 1985 it was their first National title.

- Laois once failed to register a single score when losing to Kerry in a league match (6–11 to 0–0).

- From 1950–52, and again from 1960–69, New York were automatically given a final place in an effort to promote the game in America.

- Kerry are the most successful team in the league, having played in the final on twenty-three occasions and won nineteen of these.

- Kerry also are the team to have most often achieved the 'double', winning both the league and All-Ireland Senior Football Championship.

Roll of Honour*

Kerry (19): 1928, 1929, 1931, 1932, 1959, 1961, 1963, 1969, 1971, 1972, 1973, 1974, 1977, 1982, 1984, 1997, 2004, 2006, 2009

Mayo (11): 1934, 1935, 1936, 1937, 1938, 1939, 1941, 1949, 1954, 1970, 2001

Dublin (11): 1953, 1955, 1958, 1964, 1976, 1978, 1987, 1991, 1993, 2013, 2014

Cork (8): 1952, 1956, 1980, 1989, 1999, 2010, 2011, 2012

Meath (7): 1933, 1946, 1951, 1975, 1988, 1990, 1994

Derry (6): 1947, 1992, 1995, 1996, 2000, 2008

Galway (4): 1957, 1965, 1967, 1981

Down (4): 1960, 1962, 1968, 1983

Cavan (2): 1948, 1950

Laois (2): 1926, 1986

Tyrone (2): 2002, 2003

Armagh (1): 2005

Donegal (1): 2007

Roscommon (1): 1979

Offaly (1): 1998

Monaghan (1): 1985

Longford (1): 1966

* not contested in 1927, 1930, 1940 and 1942–45

FAMOUS BAINISTEOIRS

BRIAN CODY (KILKENNY), HURLING

- Brian Cody was born on 12 July 1954 in Sheestown, County Kilkenny.

- As a player he won three All-Ireland Senior Hurling medals, four Leinster medals and two National Hurling League medals.

- Cody also captained the Kilkenny team to All-Ireland victory in 1982.

- Cody won a club All-Ireland with James Stephens as a player in 1975. They beat Blackrock of Cork to become the first Kilkenny team to take the title.

- His first All-Ireland final in charge ended in defeat to Cork by a single point.

- Cody was appointed manager of the Kilkenny senior hurling team on 16 November 1998.

- He has guided Kilkenny to nine All-Ireland wins, including four in a row (2006–09).

- 2014 is Cody's sixteenth season in charge of Kilkenny.

- In 2003 Cody's 'Cats' defeated Tipperary 5–15 to 5–13 in a thrilling league decider. He heaped more misery on the Premier County in 2009, when the 'Cats' won another league decider after extra time on a 2–26 to 4–17 scoreline. Cody then guided Kilkenny to two further league final wins against Tipperary, in 2013 and 2014.

Roll of Honour as Kilkenny manager

All-Ireland Senior Hurling Championships (9): 2000, 2002, 2003, 2006, 2007, 2008, 2009, 2011, 2012

Leinster Senior Hurling Championships (13): 1999, 2000, 2001, 2002, 2003, 2005, 2006, 2007, 2008, 2009, 2010, 2011, 2014

National Hurling League titles (8): 2002, 2003, 2005, 2006, 2009, 2012, 2013, 2014

Walsh Cup (6): 2005, 2006, 2007, 2009, 2012, 2014

Oireachtas Tournament (1): 1999

MICK O'DWYER (KERRY), FOOTBALL

– He broke both his legs playing for Kerry in 1968, yet it did not end his playing career.

– He was appointed manager of the Kerry team in 1975.

– During his twelve years as manager O'Dwyer's Kerry teams played in ten All-Ireland finals.

– Five of his players won eight Senior All-Ireland medals as O'Dwyer managed his team to eight wins in ten finals.

– From a period in 1975 to 1989, in which the

Kingdom played fifty-five championship games, they won forty-three, lost seven and drew five.

– He retired from Kerry in 1989, did two terms in Kildare, from 1991–94 and from 1998–2002, then became Laois manager in 2002.

– He led Kildare to the 1998 All-Ireland final.

Roll of Honour as manager

Kerry:

– **All-Ireland Senior Football Championships (8):** 1975, 1978, 1979, 1980, 1981, 1984, 1985, 1986

– **Munster Senior Football Championships (11):** 1975, 1976, 1977, 1978, 1979, 1980, 1981, 1982, 1984, 1985, 1986

Kildare:

– **Leinster Senior Football Championships (2):** 1998, 2000

KEVIN HEFFERNAN (DUBLIN), FOOTBALL

– He was born in Dublin on 20 August 1929.

– He won one All-Ireland medal, four Leinster medals and three National League medals as a player.

– Heffernan was an excellent hurler and won six county medals with his club, St Vincent's.

– He also won fifteen county football championship medals with St Vincent's.

– In 1963 he became the only non-player to be nominated for Texaco player of the year. His exploits as a manager and his popularity made him the outstanding choice, in a non-vintage year for players.

– He became manager of the Dublin senior inter-county team in late 1973.

– In his first championship season in charge he guided 'the Dubs' to their first Leinster title. Later that year, they added their first All-Ireland win since 1963.

Roll of Honour as Dublin manager

All-Ireland Senior Football Championships (3): 1974, 1976, 1983

Leinster Senior Football Championships (5): 1974, 1975, 1976, 1979, 1983

National Football League titles (1): 1976

SEÁN BOYLAN (MEATH), FOOTBALL

– Former team masseur, Boylan was appointed manager of Meath in 1983.

– He managed the team for a record twenty-three years.

– He retired on the evening of 31 August 2005.

- Boylan was conferred as Freeman of the County of Meath on 23 April 2006. He is the only person ever to be bestowed with the title.

- Boylan was inducted into the Leinster GAA Hall of Fame in 2006.

- Boylan had no previous managerial experience and never managed at club level.

- Boylan coached the Ireland team against Australia in the 2006 International Rules Series, and again in 2008.

Roll of Honour as Meath manager

All-Ireland Senior Football Championships (4): 1987, 1988, 1996, 1999

Leinster Senior Football Championships (8): 1986, 1987, 1988, 1990, 1991, 1996, 1999, 2001

National Football League titles (3): 1988, 1990, 1994

O'Byrne Cup (1): 1983

Centenary Cup (1): 1984

Leinster Minor Football Championship (1): 2006

GER LOUGHNANE (CLARE), HURLING

- He was born in 1953 in Feakle, County Clare.

- Loughnane never won a Munster Senior or All-Ireland senior medal in his playing career.

- He was Clare's first ever All-Star in 1974.

- He was a trainee teacher in St Patrick's College in Dublin, along with Brian Cody.

- Loughnane won two National League Hurling titles and also won Railway Cup medals in a playing career that spanned fifteen years.

- He started his managerial tuition by becoming a selector under former Tipperary great Len Gaynor.

- He reached the National League final in his first year in charge, but Clare were beaten by Kilkenny.

- Clare reached six Munster finals in seven seasons under Loughnane.

- He became manager of the Galway Senior Hurling team in 2006.

Roll of Honour as Clare manager

All-Ireland Senior Hurling Championships (2): 1995, 1997

Munster Senior Hurling Championships (3): 1995, 1997, 1998

MICKEY HARTE (TYRONE), FOOTBALL

- Born in Glencull, near Ballygawley, County Tyrone.

- Harte managed Tyrone Minors (1991–98) and Under-21s and won the All-Ireland with both these teams.

- He received an Honorary Doctorate from Queen's

University Belfast for services to Gaelic football in 2006.

– He subsequently managed his home club of Errigal Ciarán, winning the Tyrone County Championship and Ulster Championship.

– Harte was appointed Tyrone Senior football manager in 2002.

– His biography, published in October 2009, was entitled *Harte: Presence is the Only Thing*.

Roll of Honour as Tyrone manager

All-Ireland Senior Football Championships (3): 2003, 2005, 2008

Ulster Senior Football Championships (4): 2003, 2007, 2009, 2010

National Football League titles (1): 2003

Dr McKenna Cup (7): 2004, 2005, 2006, 2007, 2012, 2013, 2014

CYRIL FARRELL (GALWAY), HURLING

– He started training the Galway minor inter-county team at the age of twenty-three.

– He became Under-21 manager in 1978.

– Two years later Farrell managed Galway to its first Senior All-Ireland title since 1923.

- In 1983 he led the men from the west to a first All-Ireland title at minor level.

- He led the Galway senior hurling team to four consecutive All-Ireland final appearances from 1985–88.

- In 1987 and 1988 he steered Galway to two Senior All-Ireland victories.

Roll of Honour as Galway manager

All-Ireland Senior Hurling Championships (3): 1980, 1987, 1988

National Hurling League titles (2): 1987, 1989

MOST SUCCESSFUL INTER-COUNTY MANAGERS: ALL-IRELAND CHAMPIONSHIP HURLING WINS

Brian Cody, Kilkenny (9): 2000, 2002, 2003, 2006, 2007, 2008, 2009, 2011, 2012

Tommy Maher, Kilkenny (7): 1957, 1963, 1967, 1969, 1972, 1974, 1975

Cyril Farrell, Galway (3): 1980, 1987, 1988

Pat Henderson, Kilkenny (3): 1979, 1982, 1983

Bertie Troy, Cork (3): 1976, 1977, 1978

Dermot Healy, Offaly (2): 1981, 1985

Michael 'Babs' Keating, Tipperary (2): 1989, 1991

Ger Loughnane, Clare (2): 1995, 1997

Ollie Walsh, Kilkenny (2): 1992, 1993

MOST SUCCESSFUL INTER-COUNTY MANAGERS: ALL-IRELAND CHAMPIONSHIP FOOTBALL WINS

Mick O'Dwyer, Kerry (8): 1975, 1978, 1979, 1980, 1981, 1984, 1985, 1986

Seán Boylan, Meath (4): 1987, 1988, 1996, 1999

Jack O'Connor, Kerry (3): 2004, 2006, 2009

Mickey Harte, Tyrone (3): 2003, 2005, 2008

Kevin Heffernan, Dublin (3): 1974, 1976, 1983

Jack O'Connor, Kerry (3): 2004, 2006, 2009

Fr Tom Gilhooly, Offaly (2): 1971, 1972

Pete McGrath, Down (2): 1991, 1994

Billy Morgan, Cork (2): 1989, 1990

John O'Mahony, Galway (2): 1998, 2001

Páidí Ó Sé, Kerry (2): 1997, 2000

DUAL PLAYERS

- Teddy McCarthy of Cork is the only player in the history of the GAA to have won All-Ireland senior medals in both codes in the same season.

- McCarthy won further All-Irelands (in hurling in 1986 and in football in 1989).

- W. J. Spain was the first famous dual player. He won the first ever All-Ireland football title with Commercials of Limerick. Spain then followed up that success, capturing a hurling All-Ireland with Dublin in 1889.

- Des Ferguson and Lar Foley (Dublin) and Seán Óg Ó hAilpín (Cork) won hurling medals, but none in football.

- Greg Blaney (Down) won All-Ireland football medals, but none in hurling.

DUAL PLAYERS WITH ALL-IRELAND HURLING AND FOOTBALL MEDALS

Jimmy Barry-Murphy, Cork: Hurling 1976, 1977, 1978, 1984, 1986; Football 1973

Jack Lynch, Cork: Hurling 1941, 1942, 1943, 1944, 1946; Football 1945

Paddy Mackey, Wexford: Hurling 1910; Football 1915, 1916, 1917, 1918

Ray Cummins, Cork: Hurling 1970, 1976, 1977, 1978; Football 1973

Pierce Grace, Kilkenny and Dublin: Hurling 1911, 1912, 1913; Football 1906, 1907

Frank Burke, Dublin: Hurling 1917, 1920; Football 1921, 1922, 1923

Denis Coughlan, Cork: Hurling 1976, 1977, 1978; Football 1973

Teddy McCarthy, Cork: Hurling 1986, 1990; Football 1989, 1990

Seán O'Kennedy, Wexford: Hurling 1910; Football 1915, 1916, 1917

Brian Murphy, Cork: Hurling 1976, 1977, 1978; Football 1973

Liam Currams, Offaly: Hurling 1981; Football 1982

Billy Mackessy, Cork: Hurling 1903; Football 1911

Leonard McGrath, Galway: Hurling 1923; Football 1925

W. J. Spain, Dublin and Limerick: Football 1887; Hurling 1889

ALL-STAR AWARDS AND FAMOUS TEAMS

–   The All-Star awards began in the early 1960s. Their aim was to select the best player in each position in football and hurling, to create a team of the year.

–   Between 1963 and 1967 these players received what was known as the Cú Chulainn award.

–   In 1971 these awards were renamed the annual GAA All-Star awards.

–   In 2006 the Gaelic Players Association (GPA) launched an awards scheme of its own, entitled the GPA Gaelic Team of the Year. A yearly award was also given by the GPA to the Footballer of the Year and the Hurler of the Year. In 2011 it was announced that the GAA All-Star awards and the GPA awards would merge under the sponsorship of car manufacturer Opel. The merger was announced by GAA President Christy Cooney and it saw the achievements of players recognised jointly for the first time in October 2011.

–   Carlow and Longford are the only counties in Ireland not to have received an award in either sport.

–   In 1984, the centenary year of the GAA, a special Team of the Century was selected for hurling and football. *Sunday Independent* readers nominated players and the winners were then selected by a panel of experts and former GAA players.

- The An Post GAA Hurling Team of the Millennium was selected in 2000. The team, announced by GAA President Sean McCague on 24 July 2000 at a special function in Croke Park, was selected by a special committee comprising five past GAA presidents – Joe McDonagh, Con Murphy, Paddy Buggy, Pat Fanning and Seamus Ó Riain – as well as GAA director-general Liam Mulvihill. The four other members of the selection committee were Gaelic games journalists: Paddy Downey, Mick Dunne, Seán Óg Ó Ceallacháin and Jim O'Sullivan.

- The achievements of great Gaelic football players were also recognised with a Team of the Millennium. A special panel of past presidents and journalists selected the side.

TEAM OF THE MILLENNIUM (HURLING)

Goalkeeper:

Tony Reddin (Tipperary)

Tony Reddin was a latecomer to the game of hurling. He won both league and championship medals in 1949 and two more All-Irelands in 1950 and 1951. He also won a total of six National League medals and five Railway Cup medals. His blend of wonderful anticipation, sharp reflexes and an eagle eye made him the shot-stopper supreme.

Right full-back:

Bobby Rackard (Wexford)

He was pressed into duty at full-back when Nick O'Donnell was injured during the 1954 final against Cork. His display that day is rated as one of the best ever seen. He starred at right full-back when Wexford won the All-Irelands of 1955 and 1956. At the final whistle of the thrilling 1956 final against Cork, he and colleague Nick O'Donnell carried Christy Ring shoulder high for all to acknowledge. It remains one of the most iconic images in GAA history.

Full-back:

Nick O'Donnell (Wexford)

Nick O'Donnell was of powerful physique, but also possessed great skills. He was a defensive rock, which many a team perished upon. He captained Wexford in the 1955 final. He won a second medal in 1956 and was team captain again in 1960. His consistency led to him being named Texaco Hurler of the Year in 1960. National League honours came his way in 1956 and 1958. He was part of the famous Wexford side which overturned a fifteen point half-time deficit to win a National League final against Tipperary.

Left full-back:

John Doyle (Tipperary)

John Doyle's impressive haul of eight senior All-Ireland

hurling medals was equalled only by the legendary Christy Ring. He won his first in 1949 as a nineteen-year-old left corner-back, a position he filled again when he won in 1950 and 1951. He was a gifted and versatile hurler and he won his next two All-Ireland medals as a left half-back, before reverting to right full-back when winning his final three. He won a record ten national hurling league medals and six Railway Cup medals, and was voted Texaco Hurler of the Year in 1964. Fearless and committed, he was surely one of the true greats.

Right half-back:

Brian Whelehan (Offaly)

Brian Whelehan won minor All-Ireland medals in 1987 and 1989 as team captain. 'Sid', as he was known to his team-mates, was a stylish and tenacious player. He won Senior All-Ireland medals as a right half-back in 1994 and 1998, when his switch to attack tipped the scales in the 'Faithful's' favour. He was on the Birr team which won All-Ireland club titles in 1995 and 1998. He was selected Texaco Hurler of the Year for 1994 and again in 1998, making him the first hurler to receive such an honour for a second time.

Centre half-back:

John Keane (Waterford)

A star player in the game for seventeen seasons, he was centre back on the Waterford team which won a historic first Munster Senior Championship in 1938. A decade later he was centre forward on the Deise (Waterford) team that claimed the Liam MacCarthy Cup for the county for the first time. The Mount Sion man crowned a glittering career by winning his seventh Railway Cup medal with Munster the following season.

Left half-back:

Paddy Phelan (Kilkenny)

It was a testimony to Paddy Phelan's talent that before he ever played for his county's senior hurlers, the Leinster selectors picked him as goalkeeper on the 1930 Railway Cup team. The following season he was corner-back on the Kilkenny team that played in three classic All-Ireland finals against Cork. He was the bedrock of the Kilkenny teams that played in seven of the next nine All-Ireland finals, winning in 1932, 1933, 1935 and 1939. He was a defender in ten consecutive Railway Cup finals from 1932.

Midfield:

Lory Meagher (Kilkenny)

Lory Meagher from Tullaroan helped Leinster win the first ever Railway Cup competition in 1927, and a second six years later. He played a starring role in the first two of the 1931 epic finals against Cork, which led to him being hailed as 'a prince of hurling' and his absence through injury from the third game was a blow from which

Kilkenny couldn't recover. He did not have long to wait for national honours to come his way, as Kilkenny won the All-Irelands of 1932, 1933 and 1935 with the 'prince' displaying his wonderful range of talents.

Midfield:

Jack Lynch (Cork)

Jack Lynch was a member of a Cork side which won four All-Irelands in a row between 1941 and 1944. He captained the team of 1942. Lynch was a very skilful hurler who played at midfield. He won an All-Ireland football medal as a forward in 1945 and a year later showed his versatility by winning another All-Ireland hurling medal. He stands alone as the only player in the history of the GAA to win six consecutive senior All-Ireland medals.

Right half-forward:

Christy Ring (Cork)

Known as 'The Wizard of Cloyne', Christy Ring won a minor All-Ireland with Cork in 1938. He was the first player to win eight senior All-Ireland medals (1941–44, 1946 and 1952–54). He scored a record twenty-two goals and thirty-five points in the 1960 season, and then exceeded that total in 1961 with 104 points. The following season he shared the honour with Jimmy Doyle, with ninety-nine points each. He won his eighteenth Railway Cup medal with Munster in 1959.

Centre-forward:

Mick Mackey (Limerick)

Mick Mackey was the most famous hurler of the 1930s. In 1933 he won the Munster Championship with Limerick, before going on to lose to Kilkenny in the All-Ireland final. He then captured three Munster titles in a row, and the MacCarthy Cup in 1934, 1936 and again in 1940. He also won five National League titles in a row up to 1938. He was an integral member of Munster Railway Cup teams, winning eight times between 1934 and 1945.

Left half-forward:

Jim Langton (Kilkenny)

Jim Langton was a stylish hurler. He won his first senior medal in the famous 'Thunder and Lightning final' of 1939. He played in five more finals but won only once. He was a regular member of Leinster Railway Cup teams playing with and against the greatest players of his era – Mackey, Stokes, Rackard, Phelan and Ring.

Right corner-forward:

Jimmy Doyle (Tipperary)

At the age of fourteen Jimmy Doyle played in goal for the defeated Tipperary minors in the 1954 All-Ireland final. He went on to star as a forward in a further three minor finals. He won his first senior medal in 1958 and went on to claim five further senior medals. He was captain of the senior team in 1965. He is one of only a small number of players to win medals in three decades. He achieved the same distinction in Railway Cup hurling, winning his first of eight medals in 1958 and a final one in 1970. He won six National League titles. He was Texaco Hurler of the Year in 1965, and his amazing tally of eleven goals and ninety-one points in all competitions in 1969 made him top scorer that year.

Full-forward:

Ray Cummins (Cork)

Ray Cummins won his first senior All-Ireland in 1970 beating Wexford in what was the first eighty-minute final. His second win came as captain in 1976 and he won further medals in 1977 and 1978. He enjoyed great success with his club Blackrock, and won All-Ireland titles in 1972, 1974 and 1979. Cummins was also a superb Gaelic footballer and played at full forward on the great Cork team which took the Sam Maguire Cup in 1973. He set a unique All-Star awards record, and was honoured in both codes at the outset of the scheme in 1971; he also won further hurling awards in 1972 and 1977, and again in football in 1973.

Left corner-forward:

Eddie Keher (Kilkenny)

Eddie Keher was a member of the Kilkenny minor team in the 1959 minor final against Tipperary and made his inter-county debut as a substitute in the replayed senior final against Waterford four weeks later. He played in ten senior finals in a career that spanned eighteen years. His first of six All-Ireland senior medals came in 1963 – the others in 1967, 1969 (when he was captain), 1972, 1974 and 1975. He also won National League medals in 1962, 1966 and 1976. He was a regular on Leinster Railway Cup teams from 1961 to 1977, winning medals on nine occasions. He was selected on the first All-Star team of 1971. He was voted Texaco Hurler of the Year in 1972.

HURLING TEAM OF THE CENTURY (1984)

Goalkeeper: Tony Reddin (Tipperary); Right corner-back: Bobby Rackard (Wexford); Full-back: Nick O'Donnell (Wexford); Left corner-back: John Doyle (Tipperary); Right wing-back: Jimmy Finn (Tipperary); Centre-back: John Keane (Waterford); Left wing-back: Paddy Phelan (Kilkenny); Midfield: Lory Meagher (Kilkenny) and Jack Lynch (Cork); Right wing-forward: Christy Ring (Cork); Centre-forward: Mick Mackey (Limerick); Left wing-forward: Jim Langton (Kilkenny); Right corner-forward: Jimmy Doyle (Tipperary); Full-forward: Nicky Rackard (Wexford); Left corner-forward: Eddie Keher (Kilkenny).

TEAM OF THE MILLENNIUM (FOOTBALL)

Goalkeeper:

Dan O'Keeffe

O'Keeffe played his club football with Kerins O'Rahilly's and was a member of the Kerry senior inter-county team from 1931 until 1948. O'Keeffe is regarded as the greatest Gaelic football goalkeeper of all time. In a senior inter-county career that lasted two decades, he won every honour in the game at senior level. He was the first player to win seven All-Ireland football medals, a record which lasted until 1986. He also featured in a total of ten All-Ireland finals. He won a record fourteen Munster medals, one National Football League medal and three Railway Cup medals with Munster.

Full-back:

Joe Keohane (Kerry)

Keohane played Gaelic football with his local club John Mitchels and was a member of the Kerry senior inter-county team from 1936 to 1949. In an inter-county career that spanned two decades, Keohane won almost every honour in the game at senior level. He won five All-Ireland medals and ten Munster medals, although a National Football League title eluded him. He also won two Railway Cup medals with Munster.

Right corner-back:

Enda Colleran (Galway)

Colleran joined the senior team in the mid-1960s and was a key member of the team's three-in-a-row in 1964, 1965 and 1966. In 1967 he became only the fourth Galway player to captain a Railway Cup-winning side with Connacht. Following the end of his playing career Colleran worked as a selector with his county, and later as a manager. He managed the side to victory in the Connacht Championship in 1976. He was also an analyst on RTÉs popular show *The Sunday Game*.

Left corner-back:

Sean Flanagan (Mayo)

Flanagan captained the All-Ireland final-winning sides of 1950 and 1951 and won five Connacht Senior champion-ship medals in all. He excelled in his position and was a vital cog in the men from the West's impressive full-back line. He also won two National Football League titles in 1949 and 1954. While still a footballer, Flanagan entered into a career in politics.

Right wing-back:

Seán Murphy (Kerry)

Murphy played his club football with Dingle. His finest footballing performance was in the All-Ireland senior football final of 1959, when Kerry defeated Galway in what has become known as 'the Seán Murphy All-Ireland'. Murphy gave an outstanding display of half-back play. He was awarded the Texaco Footballer of the Year title for that year. His family was steeped in GAA tradition, and his brothers Pádraig, Seamus and Tomás also played for Kerry.

Centre-back:

J. J. O'Reilly (Cavan)

John Joe O'Reilly captained the Cavan team that won the All-Ireland Senior Football Championships in 1947 (at the New York Polo Grounds). He also played on three losing sides in finals. He won eleven Ulster senior football titles, as Cavan had a virtual monopoly from 1937 until 1949. He won a National Football League medal and four Railway Cup medals, in 1942, 1943 (when he was the first ever Cavan captain), 1947 and as captain again in 1950. O'Reilly is one of only eight men to have been presented with the Sam Maguire twice as captain. O'Reilly's father also played in goal for Cavan and his brother Tom played on the 1947 All-Ireland-winning team.

Left wing-back:

Martin O'Connell (Meath)

O'Connell won every honour in the game at senior level. He won three All-Ireland medals and claimed a record six Leinster and three National Football League titles. He has also won a host of other awards. He has been the recipient of four All-Star awards, as well as being named Texaco Footballer of the Year in his final playing season in 1996.

Midfield:

Mick O'Connell (Kerry)

O'Connell played football with local clubs Young Islanders and Waterville, and was a member of the Kerry senior inter-county team from 1956 until 1973. Known for his spectacular high fielding and long, accurate foot passing, he is a true Kingdom football legend. He won twelve Munster Senior titles and four All-Irelands, captaining the Kingdom to their 1959 Sam Maguire success. He also won four National League titles.

Midfield:

Tommy Murphy (Laois)

Murphy played his first Senior Championship match against Offaly. While he was only a sixteen-year-old schoolboy, he lined out against Kerry in the All-Ireland semi-final that same year. He won Leinster provincial medals in 1937, 1938 and 1946. In all Murphy won eight Laois Senior Club Championship medals and various Railway Cup medals for Leinster. His last game for Laois was against Wexford in the 1953 Leinster Championship and two years later he played the last game for his club, Graiguecullen. In recognition of his wonderful talent, the GAA named 'The Tommy Murphy Cup' in his honour.

Right half-forward:

Sean O'Neill (Down)

O'Neill is regarded as one of Gaelic football's most outstanding forwards, scoring eighty-five goals and over 500 points for Down in his football career. He was also a major figure in the county's All-Ireland victories of 1960, 1961 and 1968. O'Neill's career wins include eight Ulster senior football medals and eight Railway Cup medals (1960, 1963–66, 1968, 1970 and 1971). He also won three National League medals (1960, 1962 and 1968), as well as six All-Star awards. He also had a very successful college career, winning a Sigerson Cup medal with Queen's University Belfast in 1958. He later coached the university's team to further glory.

Centre half-forward:

Sean Purcell (Galway)

Purcell played college football with St Jarlath's College of Tuam. His footballing career spanned three decades – the 1940s, 1950s and 1960s. He forged what seemed like an almost telepathic on-field partnership with fellow Galway and Tuam Stars great Frank Stockwell. They became known as 'The Terrible Twins'. He won six Connacht titles and All-Ireland success came in 1956. He won a National League title and three Railway Cup medals.

Left half-forward:

Pat Spillane (Kerry)

Spillane has won the most All-Star awards to date for a footballer (nine). A dashing and exciting forward, he was also a member of the famous Kerry four-in-a-row side. He played Gaelic football with his local club Templenoe and was a vital member of the Kerry team from 1975 to 1991. While in later years he presented *The Sunday Game* and is now an analyst, it is for his on-field exploits that he will never be forgotten. He won eight All-Ireland senior medals and eleven Munster titles.

Right corner-forward:

Mikey Sheehy (Kerry)

Sheehy played Gaelic football with his local club Austin Stacks and guided them to the All-Ireland Club final against Ballerin of Derry in 1977. The Ulster champs took an early lead, but Sheehy turned out to be the hero. Two late points, one from an acute line-ball and one from a 45-metre free, gave Austin Stacks a 1–13 to 2–7 win and Sheehy a coveted All-Ireland Club winners' medal. His inter-county career was no less successful. He was a member of the Kerry senior inter-county team from 1974 until 1987 and won eight All-Ireland senior medals and three National League titles. He also won seven All-Star awards.

Full-forward:

Tommy Langan (Mayo)

Langan was born in Ballymachugh, Ballycastle, County Mayo. He joined the Mayo panel during the 1943 championship and was a regular member of the starting fifteen until his retirement following the conclusion of the 1956 championship. During that time he won two All-Ireland medals, five Connacht medals and two National League medals. Langan was seen to best effect during Mayo's golden period from 1948 to 1955, when they won five Connacht Senior Football Championships and two All-Irelands.

Left corner-forward:

Kevin Heffernan (Dublin)

Heffernan made his debut during the 1948 championship and was a regular member of the starting fifteen until his retirement after the 1962 championship. During that time he won one All-Ireland medal, four Leinster medals and three National League medals. Heffernan captained the team to the All-Ireland title in 1958. At club level Heffernan enjoyed a lengthy and very successful career with St Vincent's. He won fifteen county football championship medals and six county hurling championship medals. He would later go on to become a very successful inter-county manager.

FOOTBALL TEAM OF THE CENTURY (1984)

Goalkeeper: Dan O'Keeffe (Kerry); Right corner-back: Enda Colleran (Galway); Full-back: Paddy O'Brien (Meath); Left corner-back: Sean Flanagan (Mayo); Right half-back: Seán Murphy (Kerry); Centre-back: J. J. O'Reilly (Cavan); Left half-back: Stephen White (Louth); Midfield: Mick O'Connell (Kerry) and Jack O'Shea (Kerry); Right half-forward: Sean O'Neill (Down); Centre-forward: Sean Purcell (Galway); Left half-forward: Pat Spillane (Kerry); Right corner-forward: Mikey Sheehy (Kerry); Full-forward: Tommy Langan (Mayo); Left corner-forward: Kevin Heffernan (Dublin).

THE ALL-STAR FAMILY

Father and son

A total of nine father and son pairings have won All-Star awards. Seven of these have been in football:

– Pat Reynolds and Paddy Reynolds of Meath

– Dermot Earley and Dermot Earley Jnr of Roscommon and Kildare

– Liam O'Neill of Galway and Kevin O'Neill of Mayo

– Frank McGuigan and Brian McGuigan of Tyrone

– Bernard Brogan Sr and Alan Brogan and Bernard Brogan Jr of Dublin

– Tim Kennelly and Tadhg Kennelly of Kerry

– Martin McHugh and Mark McHugh of Donegal

The two hurling father and son pairings are:

– Fan Larkin and Philly Larkin of Kilkenny

– Richie Power Sr and Richie Power Jr of Kilkenny

All-Star brothers

Ten sets of brothers have won All-Star awards in Gaelic football. They are:

– Matt and Richie Connor of Offaly

– Tomás and Liam Connor of Offaly

– Paul and Dermot Earley Snr of Roscommon

– Seán and Brendan Lowry of Offaly

– James and Martin McHugh of Donegal

– Anthony and John McGurk of Derry

– Tom, Mick and Pat Spillane of Kerry

– Tomás, Darragh and Marc Ó Sé of Kerry

– Kenneth and Conor Mortimer of Mayo

– Alan and Bernard Brogan Jnr of Dublin

One set of brothers has won All-Star awards in hurling and football (with two different counties):

– Declan Carr won his hurling award with Tipperary and Tommy Carr won his football award while playing with Dublin.

Sixteen sets of brothers have won All-Star awards in hurling. They are:

- Tom and Jim Cashman of Cork

- Colm, Conal and Cormac Bonnar of Tipperary

- Ollie and Joe Canning of Galway

- Andy and Martin Comerford of Kilkenny

- John and Joe Connolly of Galway

- Jimmy and Joe Cooney of Galway

- Johnny, Billy and Joe Dooley of Offaly

- Colm and Tony Doran of Wexford

- Liam and Ger Fennelly of Kilkenny

- Pat, Ger and John Henderson of Kilkenny

- Eoin and Paul Kelly of Tipperary

- Willie and Eddie O'Connor of Kilkenny

- Seán Óg and Setanta Ó hAilpín of Cork

- Aidan and Bobby Ryan of Tipperary

- Martin and John Quigley of Wexford

- Jerry and Ben O'Connor (twins) of Cork

DUAL ALL-STARS

One player, Ray Cummins of Cork, has won a hurling and a football All-Star in the same year (1971). Three other players share the distinction of winning both hurling and football, but they did not win the accolades in the same year. They are:

- Liam Currams of Offaly

- Jimmy Barry-Murphy of Cork

- Brian Murphy of Cork

TOP AWARD WINNERS

- **11 awards:** Henry Shefflin (Kilkenny), hurling

- **9 awards:** Pat Spillane (Kerry), football; D. J. Carey (Kilkenny) and Tommy Walsh (Kilkenny), hurling

- **8 awards:** Colm Cooper (Kerry), football

- **7 awards:** Mikey Sheehy (Kerry), football; Noel Skehan (Kilkenny), hurling

- **6 awards:** Peter Canavan (Tyrone), Jack O'Shea (Kerry) and Ger Power (Kerry), football; Joe McKenna (Limerick), Nicky English (Tipperary), Eoin Kelly (Tipperary) and J. J. Delaney (Kilkenny), hurling

- **5 awards:** John Egan, John O'Keeffe and Páidí Ó Sé (all Kerry), John O'Leary (Dublin), Stephen Cluxton (Dublin) and Seán Cavanagh (Tyrone), football; Pat Hartigan (Limerick), Tony O'Sullivan (Cork), Joe Cooney (Galway), Joe Hennessy (Kilkenny), Eddie Keher (Kilkenny) and John Mullane (Waterford), hurling

UNIQUE ALL-STAR FACTS

– Offaly are the only team to win All-Star awards in every position, in both hurling and football.

– Damien Martin of Offaly won the first ever All-Star award.

– Paul Galvin of Kerry became the thousandth winner of the award in 2004.

– Tommy Walsh of Kilkenny has won nine hurling All-Star awards in five different positions. These were for playing at left corner-back (1), at right half-back (5), at left half-back (1), at midfield (1) and at left half-forward (1).

– Pat Spillane has won the most All-Star Football awards (9).

– Tommy Walsh is the only player to win nine successive awards.

– Pete Finnerty of Galway and Tommy Walsh of Kilkenny hold the record for most All-Star awards in the one position. Finnerty gained all his awards at right half-back.

FULL LIST OF CÚ CHULAINN/ALL-STAR AWARD WINNERS

2013 Hurling All-Stars

Anthony Nash (Cork), Richie McCarthy (Limerick), Peter Kelly (Dublin), David McInerney (Clare), Brendan Bugler (Clare), Liam Rushe (Dublin), Patrick Donnellan (Clare), Colm Galvin (Clare), Conor Ryan (Clare), Séamus Harnedy (Cork), Tony Kelly (Clare), Danny Sutcliffe (Dublin), Pádraic Collins (Clare), Patrick Horgan (Cork) and Conor McGrath (Clare).

2013 Football All-Stars

Stephen Cluxton (Dublin), Colin Walshe (Monaghan), Rory O'Carroll (Dublin), Keith Higgins (Mayo), Lee Keegan (Mayo), Cian O'Sullivan (Dublin), Colm Boyle (Mayo), Michael Darragh Macauley (Dublin), Aidan O'Shea (Mayo), Paul Flynn (Dublin), Colm Cooper (Kerry), Seán Cavanagh (Tyrone), James O'Donoghue (Kerry), Bernard Brogan (Dublin) and Conor McManus (Monaghan).

2012 Hurling All-Stars

Anthony Nash (Cork), Paul Murphy (Kilkenny), J. J. Delaney (Kilkenny), Fergal Moore (Galway), Brendan Bugler (Clare), Brian Hogan (Kilkenny), David Collins (Galway), Iarla Tannian (Galway), Kevin Moran (Waterford), T. J. Reid (Kilkenny), Henry Shefflin (Kilkenny), Damien Hayes (Galway), John Mullane (Waterford), Joe Canning (Galway) and David Burke (Galway).

2012 Football All-Stars

Paul Durcan (Donegal), Neil McGee (Donegal), Ger Cafferkey (Mayo), Keith Higgins (Mayo), Lee Keegan (Mayo), Karl Lacey (Donegal), Frank McGlynn (Donegal), Neil Gallagher (Donegal), Aidan Walsh (Cork), Paul Flynn (Dublin), Alan Dillon (Mayo), Mark McHugh (Donegal), Colm O'Neill (Cork), Michael Murphy (Donegal) and Colm McFadden (Donegal).

2011 Hurling All-Stars

Gary Maguire (Dublin), Paul Murphy (Kilkenny), Paul Curran (Tipperary), Michael Cahill (Tipperary), Tommy Walsh (Kilkenny), Brian Hogan (Kilkenny), Pádraic Maher (Tipperary), Liam Rushe (Dublin), Michael Fennelly (Kilkenny), Michael Rice (Kilkenny), Richie Power (Kilkenny), Henry Shefflin (Kilkenny), John Mullane (Waterford), Lar Corbett (Tipperary) and Richie Hogan (Kilkenny).

2011 Football All-Stars

Stephen Cluxton (Dublin), Marc Ó Sé (Kerry), Neil McGee (Donegal), Michael Foley (Kildare), Kevin Cassidy (Donegal), Karl Lacey (Donegal), Kevin Nolan (Dublin), Bryan Sheehan (Kerry), Michael Darragh Macauley (Dublin), Darran O'Sullivan (Kerry), Alan Brogan (Dublin), Paul Flynn (Dublin), Colm Cooper (Kerry), Andy Moran (Mayo) and Bernard Brogan (Dublin).

2010 Hurling All-Stars

Brendan Cummins (Tipperary), Noel Connors (Waterford),

Paul Curran (Tipperary), Jackie Tyrrell (Kilkenny), Tommy Walsh (Kilkenny), Michael Walsh (Waterford), J. J. Delaney (Kilkenny), Brendan Maher (Tipperary), Michael Fennelly (Kilkenny), Damien Hayes (Galway), Noel McGrath (Tipperary), Lar Corbett (Tipperary), John Mullane (Waterford), Richie Power (Kilkenny) and Eoin Kelly (Tipperary).

2010 Football All-Stars

Brendan McVeigh (Down), Peter Kelly (Kildare), Michael Shields (Cork), Charlie Harrison (Sligo), Paudie Kissane (Cork), Graham Canty (Cork), Philip Jordan (Tyrone), Paddy Keenan (Louth), Aidan Walsh (Cork), Daniel Hughes (Down), Martin Clarke (Down), Johnny Doyle (Kildare), Colm Cooper (Kerry), Bernard Brogan (Dublin) and Brendan Coulter (Down).

2009 Hurling All-Stars

P. J. Ryan (Kilkenny), Ollie Canning (Galway), Pádraic Maher (Tipperary), Jackie Tyrrell (Kilkenny), Tommy Walsh (Kilkenny), Michael Walsh (Waterford), Conor O'Mahony (Tipperary), Michael Rice (Kilkenny), Alan McCrabbe (Dublin), Lar Corbett (Tipperary), Henry Shefflin (Kilkenny), Eoin Larkin (Kilkenny), Noel McGrath (Tipperary), Joe Canning (Galway) and John Mullane (Waterford).

2009 Football All-Stars

Diarmuid Murphy (Kerry), Karl Lacey (Donegal), Michael Shields (Cork), Tom O'Sullivan (Kerry), Tomás Ó Sé

(Kerry), Graham Canty (Cork), John Miskella (Cork), Dermot Earley (Kildare), Seamus Scanlon (Kerry), Paul Galvin (Kerry), Pearse O'Neill (Cork), Tadhg Kennelly (Kerry), Daniel Goulding (Cork), Declan O'Sullivan (Kerry) and Stephen O'Neill (Tyrone).

2008 Hurling All-Stars

Brendan Cummins (Tipperary), Michael Kavanagh (Kilkenny), Noel Hickey (Kilkenny), Jackie Tyrrell (Kilkenny), Tommy Walsh (Kilkenny), Conor O'Mahony (Tipperary), J. J. Delaney (Kilkenny), James Fitzpatrick (Kilkenny), Shane McGrath (Tipperary), Ben O'Connor (Cork), Henry Shefflin (Kilkenny), Eoin Larkin (Kilkenny), Eddie Brennan (Kilkenny), Eoin Kelly (Waterford) and Joe Canning (Galway).

2008 Football All-Stars

Gary Connaughton (Westmeath), Conor Gormley (Tyrone), Justin McMahon (Tyrone), John Keane (Westmeath), Davy Harte (Tyrone), Tomas Ó Sé (Kerry), Philip Jordan (Tyrone), Enda McGinley (Tyrone), Shane Ryan (Dublin), Brian Dooher (Tyrone), Declan O'Sullivan (Kerry), Sean Cavanagh (Tyrone), Colm Cooper (Kerry), Kieran Donaghy (Kerry) and Ronan Clarke (Armagh).

2007 Hurling All-Stars

Brian Murray (Limerick), Michael Kavanagh (Kilkenny), Declan Fanning (Tipperary), Jackie Tyrrell (Kilkenny), Tommy Walsh (Kilkenny), Ken McGrath (Waterford),

Tony Browne (Waterford), Michael Walsh (Waterford), James Fitzpatrick (Kilkenny), Dan Shanahan (Waterford), Ollie Moran (Limerick), Stephen Molumphy (Waterford), Andrew O'Shaughnessy (Limerick), Henry Shefflin (Kilkenny) and Eddie Brennan (Kilkenny).

2007 Football All-Stars

Stephen Cluxton (Dublin), Marc Ó Sé (Kerry), Kevin McCloy (Derry), Graham Canty (Cork), Tomás Ó Sé (Kerry), Aidan O'Mahony (Kerry), Barry Cahill (Dublin), Ciaran Whelan (Dublin), Darragh Ó Sé (Kerry), Stephen Bray (Meath), Declan O'Sullivan (Kerry), Alan Brogan (Dublin), Colm Cooper (Kerry), Paddy Bradley (Derry) and Thomas Freeman (Monaghan).

2006 Hurling All-Stars

Donal Óg Cusack (Cork), Eoin Murphy (Waterford), J. J. Delaney (Kilkenny), Brian Murphy (Cork), Tony Browne (Waterford), Ronan Curran (Cork), Tommy Walsh (Kilkenny), Jerry O'Connor (Cork), James Fitzpatrick (Kilkenny), Dan Shanahan (Waterford), Henry Shefflin (Kilkenny), Eddie Brennan (Kilkenny), Eoin Kelly (Tipperary), Martin Comerford (Kilkenny) and Tony Griffin (Clare).

2006 Football All-Stars

Stephen Cluxton (Dublin), Marc Ó Sé (Kerry), Barry Owens (Fermanagh), Karl Lacey (Donegal), Seamus Moynihan (Kerry), Ger Spillane (Cork), Aidan O'Mahony

(Kerry), Darragh Ó Sé (Kerry), Nicholas Murphy (Cork), Paul Galvin (Kerry), Alan Brogan (Dublin), Alan Dillon (Mayo), Conor Mortimer (Mayo), Kieran Donaghy (Kerry) and Ronan Clarke (Armagh).

2005 Hurling All-Stars

Davy Fitzgerald (Clare), Pat Mulcahy (Cork), Diarmuid O'Sullivan (Cork), Ollie Canning (Galway), Derek Hardiman (Galway), John Gardiner (Cork), Sean Óg Ó hAilpín (Cork), Jerry O'Connor (Cork), Paul Kelly (Tipperary), Ben O'Connor (Cork), Henry Shefflin (Kilkenny), Tommy Walsh (Kilkenny), Ger Farragher (Galway), Eoin Kelly (Tipperary) and Damien Hayes (Galway).

2005 Football All-Stars

Diarmuid Murphy (Kerry), Ryan McMenamin (Tyrone), Mike McCarthy (Kerry), Andy Mallon (Armagh), Tomás Ó Sé (Kerry), Conor Gormley (Tyrone), Philip Jordan (Tyrone), Sean Cavanagh (Tyrone), Paul McGrane (Armagh), Brian Dooher (Tyrone), Peter Canavan (Tyrone), Eoin Mulligan (Tyrone), Colm Cooper (Kerry), Stephen O'Neill (Tyrone) and Steven McDonnell (Armagh).

2004 Hurling All-Stars

Damien Fitzhenry (Wexford), Wayne Sherlock (Cork), Diarmuid O'Sullivan (Cork), Tommy Walsh (Kilkenny), J. J. Delaney (Kilkenny), Ronan Curran (Cork), Seán Óg Ó hAilpín (Cork), Ken McGrath (Waterford), Jerry O'Connor (Cork), Dan Shanahan (Waterford), Niall McCarthy

(Cork), Henry Shefflin (Kilkenny), Eoin Kelly (Tipperary), Brian Corcoran (Cork) and Paul Flynn (Waterford).

2004 Football All-Stars

Diarmuid Murphy (Kerry), Tom O'Sullivan (Kerry), Barry Owens (Fermanagh), Michael McCarthy (Kerry), Tomás Ó Sé (Kerry), James Nallen (Mayo), John Keane (Westmeath), Martin McGrath (Fermanagh), Sean Cavanagh (Tyrone), Paul Galvin (Kerry), Ciaran McDonald (Mayo), Dessie Dolan (Westmeath), Colm Cooper (Kerry), Enda Muldoon (Derry) and Matty Forde (Wexford).

2003 Hurling All-Stars

Brendan Cummins (Tipperary), Michael Kavanagh (Kilkenny), Noel Hickey (Kilkenny), Ollie Canning (Galway), Seán Óg Ó hAilpín (Cork), Ronan Curran (Cork), J. J. Delaney (Kilkenny), Derek Lyng (Kilkenny), Tommy Walsh (Kilkenny), John Mullane (Waterford), Henry Shefflin (Kilkenny), Eddie Brennan (Kilkenny), Setanta Ó hAilpín (Cork), Martin Comerford (Kilkenny) and Joe Deane (Cork).

2003 Football All-Stars

Fergal Byron (Laois), Francie Bellew (Armagh), Cormac McAnallen (Tyrone), Joe Higgins (Laois), Conor Gormley (Tyrone), Tom Kelly (Laois), Philip Jordan (Tyrone), Kevin Walsh (Galway), Sean Cavanagh (Tyrone), Brian Dooher (Tyrone), Brian McGuigan (Tyrone), Declan Browne (Tipperary), Steven McDonnell (Armagh), Peter Canavan (Tyrone) and Adrian Sweeney (Donegal).

2002 Hurling All-Stars

David Fitzgerald (Clare), Michael Kavanagh (Kilkenny), Brian Lohan (Clare), Philip Larkin (Kilkenny), Fergal Healy (Waterford), Peter Barry (Kilkenny), Paul Kelly (Tipperary), Colin Lynch (Clare), Derek Lyng (Kilkenny), Eoin Kelly (Waterford), Henry Shefflin (Kilkenny), Ken McGrath (Waterford), Eoin Kelly (Tipperary), Martin Comerford (Kilkenny) and D. J. Carey (Kilkenny).

2002 Football All-Stars

Stephen Cluxton (Dublin), Enda McNulty (Armagh), Paddy Christie (Dublin), Anthony Lynch (Cork), Aidan O'Rourke (Armagh), Kieran McGeeney (Armagh), Kevin Cassidy (Donegal), Darragh Ó Sé (Kerry), Paul McGrane (Armagh), Steven McDonnell (Armagh), Eamonn O'Hara (Sligo), Oisín McConville (Armagh), Peter Canavan (Tyrone), Ray Cosgrove (Dublin) and Colm Cooper (Kerry).

2001 Hurling All-Stars

Brendan Cummins (Tipperary), Darragh Ryan (Wexford), Philip Maher (Tipperary), Ollie Canning (Galway), Eamonn Corcoran (Tipperary), Liam Hodgins (Galway), Mark Foley (Limerick), Thomas Dunne (Tipperary), Eddie Enright (Tipperary), Mark O'Leary (Tipperary), James O'Connor (Clare), Kevin Broderick (Galway), Charlie Carter (Kilkenny), Eugene Cloonan (Galway) and Eoin Kelly (Tipperary).

2001 Football All-Stars

Cormac Sullivan (Meath), Kieran Fitzgerald (Galway), Darren Fay (Meath), Coman Goggins (Dublin), Declan Meehan (Galway), Francie Grehan (Roscommon), Seán Óg de Paor (Galway), Kevin Walsh (Galway), Rory O'Connell (Westmeath), Evan Kelly (Meath), Stephen O'Neill (Tyrone), Michael Donnellan (Galway), Ollie Murphy (Meath), Pádraic Joyce (Galway) and John Crowley (Kerry).

2000 Hurling All-Stars

Brendan Cummins (Tipperary), Noel Hickey (Kilkenny), Diarmuid O'Sullivan (Cork), Willie O'Connor (Kilkenny), John Carroll (Tipperary), Eamonn Kennedy (Tipperary), Peter Barry (Kilkenny), Johnny Dooley (Offaly), Andy Comerford (Kilkenny), Denis Byrne (Kilkenny), Joe Rabbitte (Galway), Henry Shefflin (Kilkenny), Charlie Carter (Kilkenny), D. J. Carey (Kilkenny) and Joe Deane (Cork).

2000 Football All-Stars

Declan O'Keeffe (Kerry), Kieran McKeever (Derry), Seamus Moynihan (Kerry), Michael McCarthy (Kerry), Declan Meehan (Galway), Kieran McGeeney (Armagh), Anthony Rainbow (Kildare), Anthony Tohill (Derry), Darragh Ó Sé (Kerry), Michael Donnellan (Galway), Liam Hassett (Kerry), Oisín McConville (Armagh), Mike Frank Russell (Kerry), Pádraic Joyce (Galway) and Derek Savage (Galway).

1999 Hurling All-Stars

Donal Óg Cusack (Cork), Fergal Ryan (Cork), Diarmuid O'Sullivan (Cork), Frank Lohan (Clare), Brian Whelehan (Offaly), Brian Corcoran (Cork), Peter Barry (Kilkenny), Andy Comerford (Kilkenny), Tommy Dunne (Tipperary), D. J. Carey (Kilkenny), John Troy (Offaly), Brian McEvoy (Kilkenny), Sean McGrath (Cork), Joe Deane (Cork) and Niall Gilligan (Clare).

1999 Football All-Stars

Kevin O'Dwyer (Cork), Mark O'Reilly (Meath), Darren Fay (Meath), Anthony Lynch (Cork), Ciaran O'Sullivan (Cork), Kieran McGeeney (Armagh), Paddy Reynolds (Meath), John McDermott (Meath), Ciaran Whelan (Dublin), Diarmuid Marsden (Armagh), Trevor Giles (Meath), James Horan (Mayo), Philip Clifford (Cork), Graham Geraghty (Meath) and Ollie Murphy (Meath).

1998 Hurling All-Stars

Stephen Byrne (Offaly), Willie O'Connor (Kilkenny), Kevin Kinahan (Offaly), Martin Hanamy (Offaly), Anthony Daly (Clare), Sean McMahon (Clare), Kevin Martin (Offaly), Tony Browne (Waterford), Ollie Baker (Clare), Michael Duignan (Offaly), Martin Storey (Wexford), Jamsie O'Connor (Clare), Joe Dooley (Offaly), Brian Whelehan (Offaly) and Charlie Carter (Kilkenny).

1998 Football All-Stars

Martin McNamara (Galway), Brian Lacey (Kildare), Seán

Marty Lockhart (Derry), Tomás Mannion (Galway), John Finn (Kildare), Glen Ryan (Kildare), Seán Óg de Paor (Galway), Kevin Walsh (Galway), John McDermott (Meath), Michael Donnellan (Galway), Jarlath Fallon (Galway), Dermot Earley (Kildare), Karl O'Dwyer (Kildare), Padraic Joyce (Galway) and Declan Browne (Tipperary).

1997 Hurling All-Stars

Damien Fitzhenry (Wexford), Paul Shelly (Tipperary), Brian Lohan (Clare), Willie O'Connor (Kilkenny), Liam Doyle (Clare), Sean McMahon (Clare), Liam Keoghan (Kilkenny), Colin Lynch (Clare), Tommy Dunne (Tipperary), Jamsie O'Connor (Clare), Declan Ryan (Tipperary), John Leahy (Tipperary), Kevin Broderick (Galway), Ger O'Loughlin (Clare) and D. J. Carey (Kilkenny).

1997 Football All-Stars

Declan O'Keeffe (Kerry), Kenneth Mortimer (Mayo), Davy Dalton (Kildare), Cathal Daly (Offaly), Seamus Moynihan (Kerry), Glen Ryan (Kildare), Eamonn Breen (Kerry), Pat Fallon (Mayo), Niall Buckley (Kildare), Pa Laide (Kerry), Trevor Giles (Meath), Dermot McCabe (Cavan), Joe Brolly (Derry), Brendan Reilly (Meath) and Maurice Fitzgerald (Kerry).

1996 Hurling All-Stars

Joe Quaid (Limerick), Thomas Helebert (Galway), Brian Lohan (Clare), Larry O'Gorman (Wexford), Liam Dunne (Wexford), Ciaran Carey (Limerick), Mark Foley (Limerick), Adrian Fenlon (Wexford), Mike Houlihan (Limerick), Rory McCarthy (Wexford), Martin Storey (Wexford), Larry Murphy (Wexford), Liam Cahill (Tipperary), Gary Kirby (Limerick) and Tom Dempsey (Wexford).

1996 Football All-Stars

Finbarr McConnell (Tyrone), Kenneth Mortimer (Mayo), Darren Fay (Meath), Martin O'Connell (Meath), Pat Holmes (Mayo), James Nallen (Mayo), Paul Curran (Dublin), Liam McHale (Mayo), John McDermott (Meath), Trevor Giles (Meath), Tommy Dowd (Meath), James Horan (Mayo), Joe Brolly (Derry), Peter Canavan (Tyrone) and Maurice Fitzgerald (Kerry).

1995 Hurling All-Stars

Davy Fitzgerald (Clare), Kevin Kinahan (Offaly), Brian Lohan (Clare), Liam Doyle (Clare), Brian Whelehan (Offaly), Sean McMahon (Clare), Anthony Daly (Clare), Ollie Baker (Clare), Michael Coleman (Galway), Johnny Dooley (Offaly), Gary Kirby (Limerick), Jamsie O'Connor (Clare), Billy Dooley (Offaly), D. J. Carey (Kilkenny) and Ger O'Loughlin (Clare).

1995 Football All-Stars

John O'Leary (Dublin), Tony Scullion (Derry), Mark O'Connor (Cork), Fay Devlin (Tyrone), Paul Curran (Dublin), Keith Barr (Dublin), Steven O'Brien (Cork), Brian Stynes (Dublin), Anthony Tohill (Derry), Jarlath Fallon (Galway), Dessie Farrell (Dublin), Paul Clarke

(Dublin), Tommy Dowd (Meath), Peter Canavan (Tyrone) and Charlie Redmond (Dublin).

1994 Hurling All-Stars

Joe Quaid (Limerick), Anthony Daly (Clare), Kevin Kinahan (Offaly), Martin Hanamy (Offaly), Dave Clarke (Limerick), Hubert Rigney (Offaly), Kevin Martin (Offaly), Ciaran Carey (Limerick), Mike Houlihan (Limerick), Johnny Dooley (Offaly), Gary Kirby (Limerick), John Leahy (Tipperary), Billy Dooley (Offaly), D. J. Carey (Kilkenny) and Damien Quigley (Limerick).

1994 Football All-Stars

John O'Leary (Dublin), Michael Magill (Down), Seamus Quinn (Leitrim), Paul Higgins (Down), Graham Geraghty (Meath), Steven O'Brien (Cork), D. J. Kane (Down), Jack Sheedy (Dublin), Greg McCartan (Down), Peter Canavan (Tyrone), Greg Blayney (Down), James McCartan (Down), Mickey Linden (Down), Tommy Dowd (Meath) and Charlie Redmond (Dublin).

1993 Hurling All-Stars

Michael Walsh (Kilkenny), Eddie O'Connor (Kilkenny), Sean O'Gorman (Cork), Liam Simpson (Kilkenny), Liam Dunne (Wexford), Pat O'Neill (Kilkenny), Padraig Kelly (Galway), Pat Malone (Galway), Paul McKillen (Antrim), Martin Storey (Wexford), John Power (Kilkenny), D. J. Carey (Kilkenny), Michael Cleary (Tipperary), Joe Rabbitte (Galway) and Barry Egan (Cork).

1993 Football All-Stars

John O'Leary (Dublin), J. J. Doherty (Donegal), Dermot Deasy (Dublin), Tony Scullion (Derry), Johnny McGuirk (Derry), Henry Downey (Derry), Gary Coleman (Derry), Anthony Tohill (Derry), Brian McGilligan (Derry), Kevin O'Neill (Mayo), Joe Kavanagh (Cork), Charlie Redmond (Dublin), Colin Corkery (Cork), Ger Houlihan (Armagh) and Enda Gormley (Derry).

1992 Hurling All-Stars

Tommy Quaid (Limerick), Brian Corcoran (Cork), Pat Dwyer (Kilkenny), Liam Simpson (Kilkenny), Brian Whelehan (Offaly), Ciaran Carey (Limerick), Willie O'Connor (Kilkenny), M. Phelan (Kilkenny), S. McCarthy (Cork), Gerard McGrattan (Down), J. Power (Kilkenny), A. O'Sullivan (Cork), M. Cleary (Tipperary), Liam Fennelly (Kilkenny) and D. J. Carey (Kilkenny).

1992 Football All-Stars

Gary Walsh (Donegal), Seamus Clancy (Clare), Matt Gallagher (Donegal), Tony Scullion (Derry), Paul Curran (Dublin), Martin Gavigan (Donegal), Eamonn Heery (Dublin), Anthony Molloy (Donegal), T. J. Kilgallon (Mayo), Anthony Tohill (Derry), Martin McHugh (Donegal), James McHugh (Donegal), Tony Boyle (Donegal), Vinny Murphy (Dublin) and Enda Gormley (Derry).

1991 Hurling All-Stars

Michael Walsh (Kilkenny), Paul Delaney (Tipperary), Noel

Sheehy (Tipperary), Sean Treacy (Galway), Conal Bonnar (Tipperary), Jim Cashman (Cork), Chris Casey (Cork), Terence McNaughton (Antrim), John Leahy (Tipperary), Michael Cleary (Tipperary), Gary Kirby (Limerick), D. J. Carey (Kilkenny), Pat Fox (Tipperary), Cormac Bonnar (Tipperary) and John Fitzgibbon (Cork).

1991 Football All-Stars

Michael McQuillan (Meath), Mick Deegan (Dublin), Conor Deegan (Down), Enon Gavin (Roscommon), Tommy Carr (Dublin), Keith Barr (Dublin), Martin O'Connell (Meath), Barry Breen (Down), Martin Lynch (Kildare), Ross Carr (Down), Greg Blaney (Down), Tommy Dowd (Meath), Colm O'Rourke (Meath), Brian Stafford (Meath) and Bernard Flynn (Meath).

1990 Hurling All-Stars

Ger Cunningham (Cork), John Considine (Cork), Noel Sheehy (Tipperary), Sean O'Gorman (Cork), Pete Finnerty (Galway), Jim Cashman (Cork), Liam Dunne (Wexford), Michael Coleman (Galway), Johnny Pilkington (Offaly), Michael Cleary (Tipperary), Joe Cooney (Galway), Tony O'Sullivan (Cork), Eamon Morrissey (Kilkenny), Brian McMahon (Dublin) and John Fitzgibbon (Cork).

1990 Football All-Stars

John Kerins (Cork), Bobby O'Malley (Meath), Stephen O'Brien (Cork), Terry Ferguson (Meath), Michael Slo-cum (Cork), Conor Counihan (Cork), Martin O'Connell

(Meath), Shea Fahy (Cork), Mickey Quinn (Leitrim), David Beggy (Meath), Val Daly (Galway), Joyce McMullan (Donegal), Paul McGrath (Cork), Kevin O'Brien (Wicklow) and James McCartan (Down).

1989 Hurling All-Stars

John Commins (Galway), Aidan Fogarty (Offaly), Eamon Cleary (Wexford), Dessie Donnelly (Antrim), Conal Bonnar (Tipperary), Bobby Ryan (Tipperary), Sean Treacy (Galway), Michael Coleman (Galway), Declan Carr (Tipperary), Éanna Ryan (Galway), Joe Cooney (Galway), Olcan McFetridge (Antrim), Pat Fox (Tipperary), Cormac Bonnar (Tipperary) and Nicky English (Tipperary).

1989 Football All-Stars

Gabriel Irwin (Mayo), Jimmy Browne (Mayo), Gerry Hargan (Dublin), Dermot Flanagan (Mayo), Connie Murphy (Kerry), Conor Counihan (Cork), Anthony Davis (Cork), Teddy McCarthy (Cork), Willie Joe Padden (Mayo), Dave Barry (Cork), Larry Tompkins (Cork), Noel Durkin (Mayo), Paul McGrath (Cork), Eugene McKenna (Tyrone) and Tony McManus (Roscommon).

1988 Hurling All-Stars

John Commins (Galway), Sylvie Linnane (Galway), Conor Hayes (Galway), Martin Hanamy (Offaly), Pete Finnerty (Galway), Anthony Keady (Galway), Bobby Ryan (Tipperary), Colm Bonnar (Tipperary), George O'Connor (Wexford), Declan Ryan (Tipperary), Ciaran Barr (Antrim),

Martin Naughton (Galway), Martin McGrath (Galway), Nicky English (Tipperary) and Tony O'Sullivan (Cork).

1988 Football All-Stars

Paddy Linden (Monaghan), Bobby O'Malley (Meath), Colman Corrigan (Cork), Mick Kennedy (Dublin), Niall Cahalane (Cork), Noel McCaffrey (Dublin), Martin O'Connell (Meath), Shea Fahy (Cork), Liam Hayes (Meath), Maurice Fitzgerald (Kerry), Larry Tompkins (Cork), Kieran Duff (Dublin), Colm O'Rourke (Meath), Brian Stafford (Meath) and Eugene Hughes (Monaghan).

1987 Hurling All-Stars

Ken Hogan (Tipperary), Joe Hennessy (Kilkenny), Conor Hayes (Galway), Ollie Kilkenny (Galway), Pete Finnerty (Galway), Ger Henderson (Kilkenny), John Conran (Wexford), Steve Mahan (Galway), John Fenton (Cork), Martin McGrath (Galway), Joe Cooney (Galway), Aidan Ryan (Tipperary), Pat Fox (Tipperary), Nicky English (Tipperary) and Liam Fennelly (Kilkenny).

1987 Football All-Stars

John Kearns (Cork), Robbie O'Malley (Meath), Colman Corrigan (Cork), Tony Scullion (Derry), Niall Cahalane (Cork), Tom Spillane (Kerry), Ger Lynch (Kerry), Gerry McEntee (Meath), Brian McGilligan (Derry), David Beggy (Meath), Larry Tompkins (Cork), Kieran Duff (Dublin), Val Daly (Galway), Brian Stafford (Meath) and Bernard Flynn (Meath).

1986 Hurling All-Stars

Ger Cunningham (Cork), Denis Mulcahy (Cork), Conor Hayes (Galway), Sylvie Linnane (Galway), Pete Finnerty (Galway), Anthony Keady (Galway), Bobby Ryan (Tipperary), Richie Power (Kilkenny), John Fenton (Cork), Tony O'Sullivan (Cork), Tomas Mulcahy (Cork), Joe Cooney (Galway), David Kilcoyne (Westmeath), Jimmy Barry-Murphy (Cork) and Kevin Hennessy (Cork).

1986 Football All-Stars

Charlie Nelligan (Kerry), Harry Keegan (Roscommon), Mick Lyons (Meath), John Lynch (Tyrone), Tommy Doyle (Kerry), Tom Spillane (Kerry), Colm Browne (Laois), Plunkett Donaghy (Tyrone), Liam Irwin (Laois), Ray McCarron (Monaghan), Eugene McKenna (Tyrone), Pat Spillane (Kerry), Mike Sheehy (Kerry), Damien O'Hagan (Tyrone) and Ger Power (Kerry).

1985 Hurling All-Stars

Ger Cunningham (Cork), Seamus Coen (Galway), Eugene Coughlan (Offaly), Sylvie Linnane (Galway), Pete Finnerty (Galway), Pat Delaney (Offaly), Ger Coughlan (Offaly), Pat Critchley (Laois), John Fenton (Cork), Nicky English (Tipperary), Brendan Lynskey (Galway), Joe Cooney (Galway), Pat Cleary (Offaly), Padraic Horan (Offaly) and Liam Fennelly (Kilkenny).

1985 Football All-Stars

John O'Leary (Dublin), Páidí Ó Sé (Kerry), Gerry Hargan

(Dublin), Mick Spillane (Kerry), Tommy Doyle (Kerry), Ciarán Murray (Monaghan), Dermot Flanagan (Mayo), Jack O'Shea (Kerry), Willie Joe Padden (Mayo), Barney Rock (Dublin), Tommy Conroy (Dublin), Pat Spillane (Kerry), Kevin McStay (Mayo), Paul Earley (Roscommon) and Eugene Hughes (Monaghan).

1984 Hurling All-Stars

Ger Cunningham (Cork), Paudie Fitzmaurice (Limerick), Eugene Coughlan (Offaly), Pat Fleury (Offaly), Joe Hennessy (Kilkenny), John Crowley (Cork), Dermot MacCurtain (Cork), John Fenton (Cork), Joachim Kelly (Offaly), Nicky English (Tipperary), Kieran Brennan (Kilkenny), Paddy Kelly (Limerick), Tomas Mulcahy (Cork), Noel Lane (Galway) and Seanie O'Leary (Cork).

1984 Football All-Stars

John O'Leary (Dublin), Páidí Ó Sé (Kerry), Mick Lyons (Meath), Seamus McHugh (Galway), Tommy Doyle (Kerry), Tom Spillane (Kerry), P. J. Buckley (Dublin), Jack O'Shea (Kerry), Eugene McKenna (Tyrone), Barney Rock (Dublin), Eoin Liston (Kerry), Pat Spillane (Kerry), Mike Sheehy (Kerry), Frank McGuigan (Tyrone) and Dermot McNicholl (Derry).

1983 Hurling All-Stars

Noel Skehan (Kilkenny), John Henderson (Kilkenny), Leonard Enright (Limerick), Dick O'Hara (Kilkenny), Joe Hennessy (Kilkenny), Ger Henderson (Kilkenny), Tom

Cashman (Cork), Frank Cummins (Kilkenny), John Fenton (Cork), Nicky English (Tipperary), Ger Fennelly (Kilkenny), Noel Lane (Galway), Billy Fitzpatrick (Kilkenny), Jimmy Barry-Murphy (Cork) and Liam Fennelly (Kilkenny).

1983 Football All-Stars

Martin Furlong (Offaly), Páidí Ó Sé (Kerry), Stephen Kinneavy (Galway), John Evans (Cork), Pat Canavan (Dublin), Tommy Drumm (Dublin), Jimmy Kerrigan (Cork), Jack O'Shea (Kerry), Liam Austin (Down), Barney Rock (Dublin), Matt Connor (Offaly), Greg Blaney (Down), Martin McHugh (Donegal), Colm O'Rourke (Meath) and Joe McNally (Dublin).

1982 Hurling All-Stars

Noel Skehan (Kilkenny), John Galvin (Waterford), Brian Cody (Kilkenny), Pat Fleury (Offaly), Aidan Fogarty (Offaly), Ger Henderson (Kilkenny), Paddy Prendergast (Kilkenny), Tim Crowley (Cork), Frank Cummins (Kilkenny), Tony O'Sullivan (Cork), Pat Horgan (Cork), Richie Power (Kilkenny), Billy Fitzpatrick (Kilkenny), Christy Heffernan (Kilkenny) and Jim Greene (Waterford).

1982 Football All-Stars

Martin Furlong (Offaly), Mick Fitzgerald (Offaly), Liam Connor (Offaly), Kevin Kehilly (Cork), Páidí Ó Sé (Kerry), Seán Lowry (Offaly), Liam Currams (Offaly), Jack O'Shea (Kerry), Padraig Dunne (Offaly), Peter McGinnity (Fermanagh), Joe Kernan (Armagh), Matt Connor

(Offaly), Mike Sheehy (Kerry), Eoin Liston (Kerry) and John Egan (Kerry).

1981 Hurling All-Stars

Seamus Durack (Clare), Brian Murphy (Cork), Leonard Enright (Limerick), Jimmy Cooney (Galway), Liam O'Donoghue (Limerick), Sean Stack (Clare), Ger Coughlan (Offaly), Steve Mahon (Galway), Liam Currams (Offaly), John Callinan (Clare), George O'Connor (Wexford), Mark Corrigan (Offaly), Pat Carroll (Offaly), Joe McKenna (Limerick) and John Flaherty (Offaly).

1981 Football All-Stars

Martin Furlong (Offaly), Jimmy Deenihan (Kerry), Paddy Kennedy (Down), Paud Lynch (Kerry), Páidí Ó Sé (Kerry), Richie Connor (Offaly), Seamus McHugh (Galway), Jack O'Shea (Kerry), Seán Walsh (Kerry), Barry Brennan (Galway), Denis 'Ogie' Moran (Kerry), Pat Spillane (Kerry), Mike Sheehy (Kerry), Eoin Liston (Kerry) and Brendan Lowry (Offaly).

1980 Hurling All-Stars

Pat McLoughney (Tipperary), Niall McInerney (Galway), Leonard Enright (Limerick), Jimmy Cooney (Galway), Dermot McCurtain (Cork), Sean Silke (Galway), Iggy Clarke (Galway), Joachim Kelly (Offaly), Mossie Walsh (Waterford), Joe Connolly (Galway), Pat Horgan (Cork), Pat Carroll (Offaly), Bernie Forde (Galway), Joe McKenna (Limerick) and Eamon Cregan (Limerick).

1980 Football All-Stars

Charlie Nelligan (Kerry), Harry Keegan (Roscommon), Kevin Kehilly (Cork), Gerry Connellan (Roscommon), Kevin McCabe (Tyrone), Tim Kennelly (Kerry), Danny Murray (Roscommon), Jack O'Shea (Kerry), Colm McKinstry (Armagh), Ger Power (Kerry), Denis Allen (Cork), Pat Spillane (Kerry), Matt Connor (Offaly), Eoin Liston (Kerry) and John Egan (Kerry).

1979 Hurling All-Stars

Pat McLoughney (Tipperary), Brian Murphy (Cork), Martin O'Doherty (Cork), Tadhg O'Connor (Tipperary), Dermot McCurtain (Cork), Ger Henderson (Kilkenny), Iggy Clarke (Galway), John Connolly (Galway), Joe Hennessy (Kilkenny), John Callinan (Clare), Frank Burke (Galway), Liam O'Brien (Kilkenny), Mick Brennan (Kilkenny), Joe McKenna (Limerick) and 'Ned' Buggy (Wexford).

1979 Football All-Stars

Paddy Cullen (Dublin), Eugene Hughes (Monaghan), John O'Keeffe (Kerry), Tom Heneghan (Roscommon), Tommy Drumm (Dublin), Tim Kennelly (Kerry), Danny Murray (Roscommon), Dermot Earley (Roscommon), Bernard Brogan (Dublin), Ger Power (Kerry), Seán Walsh (Kerry), Pat Spillane (Kerry), Mike Sheehy (Kerry), Seán Lowry (Offaly) and Joe McGrath (Mayo).

1978 Hurling All-Stars

Seamus Durack (Clare), Phil Larkin (Kilkenny), Martin

O'Doherty (Cork), John Horgan (Cork), Joe Hennessy (Kilkenny), Ger Henderson (Kilkenny), Denis Coughlan (Cork), Tom Cashman (Cork), Iggy Clarke (Galway), Jimmy Barry-Murphy (Cork), Noel Casey (Clare), Colm Honan (Clare), Charlie McCarthy (Cork), Joe McKenna (Limerick) and Tommy Butler (Tipperary).

1978 Football All-Stars

Ollie Crinnigan (Kildare), Harry Keegan (Roscommon), John O'Keeffe (Kerry), Robbie Kelleher (Dublin), Tommy Drumm (Dublin), Ollie Brady (Cavan), Paud Lynch (Kerry), Colm McAlarney (Down), Tomás Connor (Offaly), Ger Power (Kerry), Declan Barron (Cork), Pat Spillane (Kerry), Mike Sheehy (Kerry), Jimmy Keaveney (Dublin) and John Egan (Kerry).

1977 Hurling All-Stars

Seamus Durack (Clare), John McMahon (Clare), Martin O'Doherty (Cork), John Horgan (Cork), Ger Loughnane (Clare), Mick Jacob (Wexford), Denis Coughlan (Cork), Tom Cashman (Cork), Mick Moroney (Clare), Christy Keogh (Wexford), Jimmy Barry-Murphy (Cork), P. J. Molloy (Galway), Charlie McCarthy (Cork), Ray Cummins (Cork) and Sean Ó Leary (Cork).

1977 Football All-Stars

Paddy Cullen (Dublin), Gay O'Driscoll (Dublin), Pat Lindsay (Roscommon), Robbie Kelleher (Dublin), Tommy Drumm (Dublin), Paddy Moriarty (Armagh), Pat O'Neill

(Dublin), Brian Mullins (Dublin), Joe Kernan (Armagh), Anton O'Toole (Dublin), Jimmy Smyth (Armagh), Pat Spillane (Kerry), Bobby Doyle (Dublin), Jimmy Keaveney (Dublin) and John Egan (Kerry).

1976 Hurling All-Stars

Noel Skehan (Kilkenny), Phil Larkin (Kilkenny), Willie Murphy (Wexford), John McMahon (Clare), Joe McDonagh (Galway), Mick Jacob (Wexford), Denis Coughlan (Cork), Frank Burke (Galway), Pat Moylan (Cork), Michael Malone (Cork), Martin Quigley (Wexford), Jimmy Barry-Murphy (Cork), Mick Brennan (Kilkenny), Tony Doran (Wexford) and Sean O'Leary (Cork).

1976 Football All-Stars

Paddy Cullen (Dublin), Ger O'Keeffe (Kerry), John O'Keeffe (Kerry), Brian Murphy (Cork), Johnny Hughes (Galway), Kevin Moran (Dublin), Ger Power (Kerry), Brian Mullins (Dublin), Dave McCarthy (Cork), Anton O'Toole (Dublin), Tony Hanahoe (Dublin), David Hickey (Dublin), Bobby Doyle (Dublin), Mike Sheehy (Kerry) and Pat Spillane (Kerry).

1975 Hurling All-Stars

Noel Skehan (Kilkenny), Niall McInerney (Galway), Pat Hartigan (Limerick), Brian Cody (Kilkenny), Tadhg O'Connor (Tipperary), Sean Silke (Galway), Iggy Clarke (Galway), Liam O'Brien (Kilkenny), Gerald McCarthy

(Cork), Martin Quigley (Wexford), Joe McKenna (Limerick), Eamon Grimes (Limerick), Mick Brennan (Kilkenny), Kieran Purcell (Kilkenny) and Eddie Keher (Kilkenny).

1975 Football All-Stars

Paud O'Mahony (Kerry), Gay O'Driscoll (Dublin), John O'Keeffe (Kerry), Robbie Kelleher (Dublin), Peter Stevenson (Derry), Anthony McGurk (Derry), Ger Power (Kerry), Denis Long (Cork), Colm McAlarney (Down), Gerry McElhinney (Derry), Ken Rennicks (Meath), Mickey O'Sullivan (Kerry), John Egan (Kerry), Matt Kerrigan (Meath) and Anton O'Toole (Dublin).

1974 Hurling All-Stars

Noel Skehan (Kilkenny), Phil Larkin (Kilkenny), Pat Hartigan (Limerick), John Horgan (Cork), Ger Loughnane (Clare), Pat Henderson (Kilkenny), Con Roche (Cork), Liam O'Brien (Kilkenny), John Galvin (Waterford), Joe McKenna (Limerick), Martin Quigley (Wexford), Mick Crotty (Kilkenny), John Quigley (Wexford), Kieran Purcell (Kilkenny) and Eddie Keher (Kilkenny).

1974 Football All-Stars

Paddy Cullen (Dublin), Donal Monaghan (Donegal), Seán Doherty (Dublin), Robbie Kelleher (Dublin), Paddy Reilly (Dublin), Barnes Murphy (Sligo), Johnny Hughes (Galway), Dermot Earley (Roscommon), Paud Lynch (Kerry), Tom Naughton (Galway), Declan Barron (Cork),

David Hickey (Dublin), Jimmy Barry-Murphy (Cork), Jimmy Keaveney (Dublin) and Johnny Tobin (Galway).

1973 Hurling All-Stars

Noel Skehan (Kilkenny), Phil Larkin (Kilkenny), Pat Hartigan (Limerick), Jim O'Brien (Limerick), Colm Doran (Wexford), Pat Henderson (Kilkenny), Sean Foley (Limerick), Richie Bennis (Limerick), Liam O'Brien (Kilkenny), Francis Loughnane (Tipperary), Pat Delaney (Kilkenny), Eamon Grimes (Limerick), Martin Quigley (Wexford), Kieran Purcell (Kilkenny) and Eddie Keher (Kilkenny).

1973 Football All-Stars

Billy Morgan (Cork), Frank Cogan (Cork), Mick Ryan (Offaly), Brian Murphy (Cork), Liam O'Neill (Galway), Tommy Joe Gilmore (Galway), Kevin Jer O'Sullivan (Cork), John O'Keeffe (Kerry), Denis Long (Cork), Johnny Cooney (Offaly), Kevin Kilmurray (Offaly), Liam Sammon (Galway), Jimmy Barry-Murphy (Cork), Ray Cummins (Cork) and Anthony McGurk (Derry).

1972 Hurling All-Stars

Noel Skehan (Kilkenny), Tony Maher (Cork), Pat Hartigan (Limerick), Jim Treacy (Kilkenny), Pat Lawlor (Kilkenny), Mick Jacob (Wexford), Con Roche (Cork), Frank Cummins (Kilkenny), Denis Coughlan (Cork), Francis Loughnane (Tipperary), Pat Delaney (Kilkenny), Eddie Keher (Kilkenny), Charlie McCarthy (Cork), Ray Cummins (Cork) and Eamon Cregan (Limerick).

1972 Football All-Stars

Martin Furlong (Offaly), Mick Ryan (Offaly), Paddy McCormack (Offaly), Donie O'Sullivan (Kerry), Brian McEniff (Donegal), Tommy Joe Gilmore (Galway), Kevin Jer O'Sullivan (Cork), Willie Bryan (Offaly), Mick O'Connell (Kerry), Johnny Cooney (Offaly), Kevin Kilmurray (Offaly), Tony McTague (Offaly), Mickey Freyne (Roscommon), Sean O'Neill (Down) and Paddy Moriarty (Armagh).

1971 Hurling All-Stars

Damien Martin (Offaly), Tony Maher (Cork), Pat Hartigan (Limerick), Jim Treacy (Kilkenny), Tadhg O'Connor (Tipperary), Mick Roche (Tipperary), Martin Coogan (Kilkenny), John Connolly (Galway), Frank Cummins (Kilkenny), Francis Loughnane (Tipperary), Michael Keating (Tipperary), Eddie Keher (Kilkenny), Mick Bermingham (Dublin), Ray Cummins (Cork) and Eamon Cregan (Limerick).

1971 Football All-Stars

P. J. Smyth (Galway), Johnny Carey (Mayo), Jack Cosgrove (Galway), Donie O'Sullivan (Kerry), Eugene Mulligan (Offaly), Nicholas Clavin (Offaly), Pat Reynolds (Meath), Liam Sammon (Galway), Willie Bryan (Offaly), Tony McTague (Offaly), Ray Cummins (Cork), Mickey Kearns (Sligo), Andy McCallin (Antrim), Sean O'Neill (Down) and Seamus Leydon (Galway).

CÚ CHULAINN AWARD WINNERS (FOOTBALL)

1963 Cú Chulainn Awards

Andy Phillips (Wicklow), Gabriel Kelly (Cavan), Noel Tierney (Galway), Pa Connolly (Kildare), Seamus Murphy (Kerry), Paddy Holden (Dublin), Martin Newell (Galway), Mick Garrett (Galway), Des Foley (Dublin), Sean O'Neill (Down), Mickey Whelan (Dublin), Tom Browne (Laois), Jimmy Whan (Armagh), Tom Long (Kerry), Pat Donnellan (Galway) and Lar Foley (Dublin).

1964 Cú Chulainn Awards

Johnny Geraghty (Galway), Gabriel Kelly (Cavan), Noel Tierney (Galway), Peter Darby (Meath), Enda Colleran (Galway), Paddy Holden (Dublin), Frank Lynch (Louth), Mick O'Connell (Kerry), Mick Reynolds (Galway), Cyril Dunne (Galway), Mattie McDonagh (Galway), Mickey Kearns (Sligo), Sean O'Neill (Down), Charlie Gallagher (Cavan) and Paddy Doherty (Down).

1965 Cú Chulainn Awards

Johnny Geraghty (Galway), Enda Colleran (Galway), Tom McCreesh (Armagh), Bosco McDermott (Galway), Donie O'Sullivan (Kerry), Paddy Holden (Dublin), Martin Newell (Galway), Mick O'Connell (Kerry), Des Foley (Dublin), Cyril Dunne (Galway), Mickey Kearns (Sligo), Seamus Leydon (Galway), Sean Murray (Longford), Sean O'Neill (Down) and Paddy Doherty (Down).

1966 Cú Chulainn Awards

Johnny Geraghty (Galway), Enda Colleran (Galway), Jack Quinn (Meath), Peter Darby (Meath), Pat Collier (Meath), Mick Carolan (Kildare), Brendan Barden (Longford), Pat Donnellan (Galway), Ray Carolan (Cavan), Mickey Kearns (Sligo), Mattie McDonagh (Galway), Seamus Leydon (Galway), Pat Dunny (Kildare), Con O'Sullivan (Cork) and John Keenan (Galway).

1967 Cú Chulainn Awards

Billy Morgan (Cork), Gabriel Kelly (Cavan), Jack Quinn (Meath), Seamus O'Connor (Mayo), Frank Cogan (Cork), Bertie Cunningham (Meath), Pat Reynolds (Meath), Mick Burke (Cork), Ray Carolan (Cavan), Cyril Dunne (Galway), Joe Langan (Mayo), Joe Corcoran (Mayo), Sean O'Connell (Derry), Con O'Sullivan (Cork) and Sean O'Neill (Down).

CÚ CHULAINN AWARD WINNERS (HURLING)

1963 Cú Chulainn Awards

Ollie Walsh (Kilkenny), Tom Neville (Wexford), Austin Flynn (Waterford), John Doyle (Tipperary), Séamus Cleere (Kilkenny), Billy Rackard (Wexford), Larry Guinan (Waterford), Theo English (Tipperary), Des Foley (Dublin), Jimmy Doyle (Tipperary), Mick Flannelly (Waterford), Eddie Keher (Kilkenny), Liam Devaney (Tipperary), Jimmy Smyth (Clare) and Phil Grimes (Waterford).

1964 Cú Chulainn Awards

Ollie Walsh (Kilkenny), John Doyle (Tipperary), Pa Dillon (Kilkenny), Tom Neville (Wexford), Séamus Cleere (Kilkenny), Tony Wall (Tipperary), Pat Henderson (Kilkenny), Mick Roche (Tipperary), Paddy Moran (Kilkenny), Jimmy Doyle (Tipperary), Michael 'Babs' Keating (Tipperary), Eddie Keher (Kilkenny), Tom Walsh (Kilkenny), John McKenna (Tipperary) and Donie Nealon (Tipperary).

1965 Cú Chulainn Awards

John O'Donoghue (Tipperary), Tom Neville (Wexford), Austin Flynn (Waterford), Kieran Carey (Tipperary), Denis O'Riordan (Cork), Tony Wall (Tipperary), Jimmy Duggan (Galway), Phil Wilson (Wexford), Mick Roche (Tipperary), Jimmy Doyle (Tipperary), Pat Carroll (Kilkenny), Pat Cronin (Clare), Donie Nealon (Tipperary), John McKenna (Tipperary) and Seán McLoughlin (Tipperary).

1966 Cú Chulainn Awards

Paddy Barry (Cork), Pat Henderson (Kilkenny), Austin Flynn (Waterford), Denis Murphy (Cork), Séamus Cleere (Kilkenny), Kevin Long (Limerick), Martin Coogan (Kilkenny), Bernie Hartigan (Limerick), Theo English (Tipperary), Seánie Barry (Cork), Eddie Keher (Kilkenny), Pat Cronin (Clare), Paddy Molloy (Offaly), John McKenna (Tipperary) and Mattie Fox (Galway). Justin McCarthy (Cork) won 1966 Hurler of the Year but got no Cú Chulainn Award.

1967 Cú Chulainn Awards

Ollie Walsh (Kilkenny), Pat Henderson (Kilkenny), Pa Dillon (Kilkenny), Jim Treacy (Kilkenny), Séamus Cleere (Kilkenny), Jimmy Cullinan (Clare), Len Gaynor (Tipperary), Mick Roche (Tipperary), Paddy Moran (Kilkenny), Eddie Keher (Kilkenny), Tony Wall (Tipperary), Pat Cronin (Clare), Donie Nealon (Tipperary), Tony Doran (Wexford) and Michael 'Babs' Keating (Tipperary).

MUNSTER MILLENNIUM HURLING TEAM*

Tony Reddin (Tipperary), John Doyle (Tipperary), Brian Lohan (Clare), Denis Murphy (Cork), Jimmy Finn (Tipperary), John Keane (Waterford), Jackie Power (Limerick), Jack Lynch (Cork), Phil Grimes (Waterford), Jimmy Doyle (Tipperary), Mick Mackey (Limerick), Christy Ring (Cork), Jimmy Smyth (Clare), Ray Cummins (Cork) and Paddy Barry (Cork).

* The *Cork Examiner* asked a panel of former hurlers and journalists to select both teams of the millennium from Munster.

MUNSTER MILLENNIUM FOOTBALL TEAM

Billy Morgan (Cork), Paddy O'Driscoll (Cork), John O'Keeffe (Kerry), Donie O'Sullivan (Kerry), Páidí Ó Sé (Kerry), Bill Casey (Kerry), Niall Cahalane (Cork), Mick O'Connell (Kerry), Jack O'Shea (Kerry), Packie Brennan (Tipperary), Larry Tompkins (Cork), Pat Spillane (Kerry), Michael Sheehy (Kerry), Eoin Liston (Kerry) and John Egan (Kerry).

CORK FOUR-IN-A-ROW HURLING TEAM (1944)

T. Mulcahy, W. Murphy, B. Thornhill, D. J. Buckley, P. O'Donovan, C. Murphy, A. Lotty, J. Lynch, C. Cottrell, C. Ring, S. Condon (capt.), J. Young, J. Quirke, J. Morrison and J. Kelly. Sub: P. Healy for C. Murphy.

KILKENNY FOUR-IN-A-ROW HURLING TEAM (2009)

P. J. Ryan, M. Kavanagh, J. J. Delaney, J. Tyrrell, T. Walsh, B. Hogan, J. Tennyson, D. Lyng, M. Rice, E. Brennan, E. Larkin, R. Power, R. Hogan, H. Shefflin and A. Fogarty. Subs: T. J. Reid for A. Fogarty, M. Fennelly (capt.) for D. Lyng, M. Comerford for R. Hogan.

WEXFORD FOUR-IN-A-ROW FOOTBALL TEAM (1918)

T. McGrath, N. Stuart, P. Mackey, J. Byrne (capt.), T. Murphy, T. Doyle, M. Howlett, W. Hodgins, J. Doran, J. Crowley, R. Reynolds, T. Pierse, A. Doyle, G. Kennedy and J. Redmond.

KERRY FOUR-IN-A-ROW FOOTBALL TEAM (1932)

D. O'Keeffe, D. O'Connor, Joe Barrett (capt.), Jack Walsh, P. Russell, Joe O'Sullivan, P. Whitty, R. Stack, J. Walsh, C. Geaney, M. Doyle, T. Landers, J. Ryan, C. Brosnan and J. J. Landers. Sub: W. Landers for C. Geaney.

KERRY FOUR-IN-A-ROW FOOTBALL TEAM (1981)

C. Nelligan, J. Deenihan (capt.), J. O'Keeffe, P. Lynch, P. Ó Sé, T. Kennelly, M. Spillane, S. Walsh, J. O'Shea, G. Power, D. 'Ogie' Moran, T. Doyle, M. Sheehy, E. Liston and J. Egan. Subs: P. Spillane for J. Egan, G. O'Keeffe for M. Spillane.

TIPPERARY (THURLES) FIRST ALL-IRELAND HURLING CHAMPIONS (1887)

Jim Stapleton (capt.), Matty Maher, Tom Maher, Andy Maher, Tom Burke, Martin McNamara, Ned Murphy, Jer Dwyer, Tom Stapleton, Ned Bowe, Tom Healy, Dan Ryan, Ger Ryan, Pat Leahy, Tim Dwyer, Jack Mockler, Jack Dunne, Tom Carroll, John Leamy, Mick Carroll and Ned Lambe.

CUPS AND TROPHIES

SAM MAGUIRE CUP

This famous trophy is awarded to the winners of the All-Ireland Senior Football Championship. It is modelled on the Ardagh Chalice and cost £300. The trophy bears the name of Sam Maguire, who was born in Dunmanway, Co. Cork, in 1879. At the age of twenty he started working for the postal service in London and became very active in the GAA there. He was a member of the Hibernians club and played with London in the All-Ireland football finals of 1900, 1901 (capt.) and 1902. He was also a member of the Irish Republican Brotherhood and brought Michael Collins into that organisation. In December 1924 he returned to Dunmanway. He died in 1927.

The trophy was presented to the GAA by friends and former colleagues in 1928. The first winners were Kildare, who beat Cavan in the final. It was taken out of circulation in 1988 and the replacement replica trophy was first won by Meath, who beat Cork in that year's final. The Meath men had also beaten Cork the previous year, so they were the last winners of the original as well.

LIAM MACCARTHY CUP

The trophy is awarded to the winners of the All-Ireland Senior Hurling Championship. It is named after former London GAA treasurer and chairman Liam MacCarthy.

He was born in London in 1851 to Irish parents. He was appointed the first treasurer of the London association and became president three years later.

The trophy which bears his name was presented to the Central Council in 1921. The first winners were Limerick, who beat Dublin in the delayed final played in May 1923. This cup was 'retired' in 1992 to be replaced by an exact replica, which was first won by Kilkenny who beat Cork in the final.

THE TOMMY MARKHAM CUP

Presented to the winning county of the ESB GAA Football All-Ireland Minor Championship. The cup commemorates the late Tom Markham, a Clare man who gave great service to the GAA. It was first presented at the 1940 All-Ireland final, when Louth were victorious.

IRISH PRESS CUP

Presented to the winners of the All-Ireland Minor Hurling Championship.

NEW IRELAND CUP

Awarded to the winners of the National Football League.

DR CROKE CUP

Awarded to the winners of the National Hurling League. The competitions are called the Allianz Leagues for sponsorship reasons.

ANDY MERRIGAN CUP

Awarded to the winners of the All-Ireland Senior Club Football Championship. The All-Ireland Club championships began in 1971, but the first winners of this trophy were UCD in 1974.

TOMMY MOORE CUP

Awarded to the winners of the All-Ireland Club Hurling Championship. A native of Ballyragget, Co. Kilkenny, Tommy Moore was prominently associated with the Faughs club in Dublin for most of his adult life.

CLARKE CUP

The cup is presented to the winners of the Under-21 Football Championship.

J. J. NESTOR CUP

This trophy is awarded to the winners of the Connacht Senior Football Championship. It is named after former Dunmore McHales club player and Galway chairman J. J. Nestor.

BOB O'KEEFFE CUP

Awarded to the winners of the Leinster Senior Hurling Championship. It is named after former GAA president Robert O'Keeffe.

LIAM HARVEY CUP

This trophy is awarded to the winners of the Ulster Senior Hurling Championship.

M. J. 'INKY' FLAHERTY CUP

Formerly awarded to the winners of the Connacht Senior Hurling Championship, it is no longer contested.

DELANEY CUP

The Delaney cup is presented to the winners of the Leinster Senior Football Championship and named after a famous GAA family from Laois.

MUNSTER SENIOR FOOTBALL CHAMPIONSHIP

Awarded to the winners of the Munster Senior Football Championship. The cup is named after the championship in Munster and unlike many GAA cups has no distinctive name.

MUNSTER SENIOR HURLING CUP

Like the Munster football competition, the cup is named after the championship itself.

CHRISTY RING CUP

The cup commemorates one of hurling's greatest ever exponents. It is presented to the winners of Senior hurling's second tier.

NICKY RACKARD CUP

Named after Wexford legend Nicky Rackard, this is presented to the winner of the third tier competition for Senior hurling.

LORY MEAGHER CUP

This cup is presented to the winners of the fourth tier in Senior hurling. It is named after former Kilkenny great Lory Meagher.

ANGLO-CELT CUP

Awarded to the winners of the Ulster Senior Football Championship. It was first won by Monaghan in 1888.

THE CROSS OF CASHEL

This trophy is awarded to the winners of the All-Ireland Under-21 Hurling Championship.

HOGAN CUP

Awarded to the winners of All-Ireland Colleges' Football.

SIGERSON CUP

This famous trophy is awarded to the winners of the Third-Level Football Championship.

CROKE CUP

This cup is presented to the winners of the All-Ireland Colleges' Hurling and should not be confused with the Dr Croke cup.

FITZGIBBON CUP

This trophy is presented to the winners of the Third-Level Hurling Championship.

DR HARTY CUP

Awarded to the winners of the senior schools hurling competition in Munster.

O'DUFFY CUP

Presented to the winner of the All-Ireland Camogie championship at senior level. It is named after a former member of the Kilmacud Crokes club in Dublin.

JACK MCGRATH CUP

This cup is presented to the winners of the intermediate grade in camogie. The competition replaced the All-Ireland Senior B Championship. Jack McGrath from Crosshaven, Co. Cork, a well-known referee and former chairman of the Carrigdhoun Board, donated the cup.

KAY MILLS CUP

The winners of the All-Ireland Junior Camogie title are presented with this trophy. It is named after former Dublin star Kay Mills.

NANCY MURRAY CUP

This cup is named after Anne 'Nancy' Mulligan-Murray from Antrim. She was the sixteenth president of the Camogie Association. The competition is for the fourth tier of camogie and began in 2007.

BRENDAN MARTIN CUP

This trophy is presented to the winners of the All-Ireland Ladies championship in Senior football. It is named after Brendan Martin, a native of Tullamore in County Offaly and one of the founders of the Ladies Football Association.

MARY QUINN MEMORIAL CUP

This cup is presented to the winners of the Ladies inter-mediate football competition. The first final was con-tested in 1991.

INTERNATIONAL RULES SERIES

–   The International Rules Series is an international tournament between the Australian international rules football team and the Irish international rules football team.

–   The series has been tried in a number of formats over the years. It is held after the completion of the Australian AFL Grand Final and the All-Ireland football final, which are both traditionally played in late September.

–   The two teams compete for a trophy, which in 2004 was named in honour of Cormac McAnallen. The former Tyrone team captain had died that year from a heart condition. He had been an integral member of the Irish side in the previous three series.

–   The series began in Ireland in 1984 under a three-match format, and the team that accumulated the majority of wins were awarded the victory.

–   The International Rules Series matches use a mixture of rules from both codes, but the size of field and the ball are both taken from Gaelic football. Australian rules is played with an oval ball and on a much bigger pitch.

–   Kevin 'Heffo' Heffernan managed Ireland to victory

over Australia in the International Rules Series in 1986.

- Following poor Australian crowds and relative lack of interest, the competition was shelved in 1990.

- The series was revived in 1998 under a two-match format with victory awarded on an aggregate points system.

- Michael O'Loughlin was the star of the series in 2000. His seventeen-point haul in the final test was the difference between the sides. The man with the Irish-sounding name was actually Aboriginal and an AFL star with the Sidney Swans.

- Australia overturned a nineteen points deficit at half-time, to win by seven, 65–58 in the opening game of the 2002 series. This win would prove to be decisive, as the second test ended in a tie, 42–42.

- There have only ever been two draws in a test match. The second test in 1999 and the second test in 2002.

- Only once has any test sold out in Australia – in Perth in 2003.

- The first series to sell out was in Ireland in 2006, when a combined record crowd of 112,127 attended.

- The tests were postponed by the GAA in 2007 following the 2006 series, when a number of violent on-field incidents occurred.

- The series was revived in October 2008 in Australia, after the GAA and AFL reached agreement on a revised set of rules.

- Steven McDonald of Armagh is the series all-time top scorer, with 118 points.

- The 2013 series was the first time an Australian team was made up of exclusively indigenous players, known as the Indigenous All-Stars.

- The 2014 series will be a one-off test to be held in Patersons Stadium in Perth on Saturday 22 November.

ALL-TIME SERIES STANDINGS

	Series wins	Test wins	Points scored
Ireland	9	20	2,166
Australia	8	16	2,013

Two draws (second test 1999, second test 2002)

SERIES RECORDS

Biggest series win: 101 points in 2013, Ireland 173–72 Australia

Biggest test win: 79 points in the second test 2013, Ireland 116–37 Australia

Closest series: 5 points in 2008, Ireland 102–97 Australia

Highest-scoring test: 164 points in the first test 2005, Australia 100–64 Ireland

Lowest-scoring test: 84 points in the second test 2002, Ireland 42–42 Australia

Highest attendance: 82,127, Croke Park, second test 2006

Lowest attendance: 7,000, Bruce Stadium, second test 1990

SERIES RESULTS

Scores are given in the form goals–overs–behinds (points). A goal equals 6 points, an over 3, and a behind 1.

2013

Ireland 2–12–9 (57), Australia 1–7–8 (35), Breffni Park, Cavan.

Ireland 6–22–14 (116), Australia 2–7–4 (37), Croke Park, Dublin.

Series final score: Ireland 173, Australia 72.

2011

Ireland 4–17–5 (80), Australia 1–8–6 (36), Etihad Stadium, Melbourne.

Ireland 1–13–5 (50), Australia 0–7–8 (29), Metricon Stadium, Gold Coast.

Series final score: Ireland 130, Australia 65.

2010

Australia 0–14–5 (47), Ireland 1–8–10 (40), Gaelic Grounds, Limerick.

Australia 0–14–13 (55), Ireland 1–11–13 (52), Croke Park, Dublin.

Series final score: Australia 102, Ireland 92.

2008

Ireland 3–6–9 (45), Australia 0–12–8 (44), Subiaco Oval, Perth.

Ireland 4–8–9 (57), Australia 3–8–11 (53), MCG, Melbourne.

Series final score: Ireland 102, Australia 97.

2006

Ireland 1–12–6 (48), Australia 1–9–7 (40), Pearse Stadium, Galway.

Australia 3–15–6 (69), Ireland 0–7–10 (31), Croke Park, Dublin.

Series final score: Australia 109, Ireland 79.

2005

Australia 2–27–7 (100), Ireland 3–11–13 (64), Subiaco Oval, Perth.

Australia 0–18–9 (63), Ireland 0–11–9 (42), Telstra Dome, Melbourne.

Series final score: Australia 163, Ireland 106.

2004

Ireland 3–17–8 (77), Australia 1–9–8 (41), Croke Park, Dublin.

Ireland 1–15–4 (55), Australia 0–12–5 (41), Croke Park, Dublin.

Series final score: Ireland 132, Australia 82.

2003

Australia 3–10–8 (56), Ireland 1–10–10 (46), Subiaco Oval, Perth.

Ireland 2–9–9 (48), Australia 1–10–9 (45), MCG, Melbourne.

Series final score: Australia 101, Ireland 94.

2002

Australia 2–15–8 (65), Ireland 1–14–10 (58), Croke Park, Dublin.

Ireland 1–8–12 (42), Australia 1–11–3 (42), Croke Park, Dublin.

Series final score: Australia 107, Ireland 100.

2001

Ireland 2–13–8 (59), Australia 1–13–8 (53), MCG, Melbourne.

Ireland 2–17–8 (71), Australia 1–13–7 (52), Football Park, Adelaide.

Series final score: Ireland 130, Australia 105.

2000

Australia 0–14–13 (55), Ireland 1–11–8 (47), Croke Park, Dublin.

Australia 2–15–11 (68), Ireland 1–12–9 (51), Croke Park, Dublin.

Series final score: Australia 123, Ireland 98.

1999

Ireland 2–16–10 (70), Australia 0–15–17 (62), MCG, Melbourne.

Ireland 1–11–13 (52), Australia 2–12–4 (52), Football Park, Adelaide.

Series final score: Ireland 122, Australia 114.

1998

Australia 2–12–14 (62), Ireland 2–12–13 (61), Croke Park, Dublin.

Ireland 4–12–7 (67), Australia 2–10–14 (56), Croke Park, Dublin.

Series final score: Ireland 128, Australia 118.

1990

Ireland 0–12–11 (47), Australia 0–10–8 (38), VFL Park, Victoria.

Ireland 3–9–7 (52), Australia 0–7–10 (31), Canberra Stadium.

Australia 0–13–11 (50), Ireland 0–12–8 (44), WACA Ground, Perth.

Series final score: Ireland 143, Australia 119.

1987

Ireland 3–7–14 (53), Australia 1–11–12 (51), Croke Park, Dublin.

Australia 3–14–12 (72), Ireland 3–6–11 (47), Croke Park, Dublin.

Australia 0–14–17 (59), Ireland 1–13–10 (55), Croke Park, Dublin.

Series final score: Australia 182, Ireland 155.

1986

Australia 1–14–16 (64), Ireland 5–5–12 (57), WACA Ground, Perth.

Ireland 3–10–14 (62), Australia 1–10–10 (46), VFL Park, Victoria.

Ireland 4–8–7 (55), Australia 0–7–11 (32), Football Park, Adelaide.

Series final score: Ireland 174, Australia 142.

1984

Australia 2–15–13 (70), Ireland 4–8–9 (57), Páirc Uí Chaoimh, Cork.

Ireland 3–18–8 (80), Australia 1–18–16 (76), Croke Park, Dublin.

Australia 1–18–16 (76), Ireland 5–11–8 (71), Croke Park, Dublin.

Series final score: Australia 222, Ireland 208.

LIST OF VENUES

Breffni Park (Cavan, Ulster)

Canberra (Bruce) Stadium (Canberra, Australian Capital Territory)

Carrara Stadium (Gold Coast, Queensland), also called Metricon.

Croke Park (Dublin, Leinster)

Docklands Stadium (Melbourne, Victoria), also known by the names Telstra Dome, and now Etihad Stadium.

Football Park (Adelaide, South Australia)

Gaelic Grounds (Limerick, Munster)

Melbourne Cricket Ground (MCG) (Melbourne, Victoria)

Páirc Uí Chaoimh (Cork, Munster)

Pearse Stadium (Galway, Connacht)

Subiaco Oval (Perth, Western Australia)

WACA Ground (Perth, Western Australia)

VFL Park (Mulgrave, Victoria), now known as Waverley Park.

PLAYER AWARDS

GAA Medal

The GAA Medal (also known as the Irish Player of the Series) is awarded to the outstanding Irish player of the series. It has been awarded since 2004.

2004: Stephen Cluxton (Dublin)

2005: Tom Kelly (Laois)

2006: Alan Brogan (Dublin)

2008: Graham Canty (Cork)

2010: Colm Begley (Laois)

2011: Tadhg Kennelly (Kerry/Sydney Swans)

2013: Not awarded

Jim Stynes Medal

The Jim Stynes Medal is awarded to the outstanding Australian player for each series. It was first awarded in 1998 and named after Jim Stynes, former Dublin Gaelic footballer and Melbourne AFL star. Stynes was the first overseas player to win the Brownlow Medal (the highest individual AFL honour) and was inducted into the AFL Hall of Fame in 2003. He also set a record for the most consecutive games played (244). He died in 2012.

1998: Stephen Silvagni (Carlton)

1999: Jason Akermanis (Brisbane)

2000: James Hird (Essendon)

2001: Matthew Lloyd (Essendon)

2002: Andrew Kellaway (Richmond)

2003: Brent Harvey (North Melbourne)

2004: Nathan Brown (Richmond)

2005: Andrew McLeod (Adelaide)

2006: Ryan O'Keefe (Sydney)

2008: Kade Simpson (Carlton)

2010: Dane Swan (Collingwood)

2011: James Kelly (Geelong)

2013: Ashley McGrath (Brisbane)

Harry Beitzel Medal

The Harry Beitzel Medal is a fair play award. It was awarded under the criteria that the highest standard of fair play had been attained. The medal was presented between 1984 to 1990. Beitzel was honoured for his pioneering work within the sport. He also arranged the first ever official contact between the two sports of Gaelic and Australian rules football.

1984: Jimmy Kerrigan (Ireland)

1986: Robert DiPierdomenico (Australia)

1987: Tony McGuinness (Australia)

1990: Jack O'Shea (Ireland)

SCHOOLS, COLLEGES AND UNIVERSITIES

THE SIGERSON CUP

- The cup is named after Dr George Sigerson, who was a professor of zoology at University College Dublin. In 1911 he offered to donate a trophy for an intervarsity competition.

- The cup is in the shape of a mether, an ancient Irish drinking vessel, and has four handles representing the four provinces.

- The first winning captain was W. J. O'Riordan, who received the cup on behalf of UCC, the first winning team.

- In 2009 Sigerson was named in the *Sunday Tribune*'s list of 'the 125 Most Influential People in GAA History'. The trophy itself is the longest-serving trophy in national circulation in Gaelic games. The original was replaced by an exact replica in 2001.

- UCD have dominated the competition, winning thirty-two titles. Their greatest era was the 1970s, when they won the title six times in seven years. These wins provided UCD with the platform to go on and win two All-Ireland Club Championships.

- Henry Kenny (UCG & Mayo), father of Taoiseach Enda Kenny, was a six-time medallist with UCG from 1936–37 to 1941–42.

- Mick Raftery (UCG & Mayo/Galway) has a record eight Sigerson wins (between 1933–34 and 1941–42).

- Frank Burke (UCD & Kildare/Dublin) holds the record of winning the most intervarsity honours, his nine victories comprising five in the Sigerson Cup and four in the Fitzgibbon Cup.

- The early years saw only three teams taking part: UCD, UCC and UCG. The competition has been run every year since, except in 1920–21 and 1942–43.

- UCG and UCC are second in the all-time winners' list, currently having twenty-two victories each to their credit. After their victory in 1936–37, the Galway University club went on to claim the next five titles, and this six-in-a-row haul is the longest unbroken sequence in the competition.

- Trinity College Dublin first entered in 1963, followed by NUIM in 1972.

- In the 1990s the competition expanded further, with the admission of Regional Technical Colleges to the competition.

- All of these third-level institutions have won the Sigerson Cup since the mid-nineties, the most recent being DIT in 2013.

Roll of Honour*

University College Dublin (32): 1913, 1915, 1917, 1918, 1920, 1924, 1927, 1929, 1930, 1931, 1932, 1933, 1936,

1945, 1946, 1948, 1950, 1954, 1956, 1957, 1958, 1960, 1962, 1968, 1973, 1974, 1975, 1977, 1978, 1979, 1985, 1996

National University of Ireland, Galway (formerly UCG) (22): 1912, 1922, 1934, 1935, 1937, 1938, 1939, 1940, 1941, 1942, 1949, 1951, 1955, 1961, 1963, 1964, 1980, 1981, 1983, 1984, 1992, 2003

University College Cork (22): 1911, 1914, 1916, 1919, 1923, 1925, 1926, 1928, 1944, 1947, 1952, 1953, 1966, 1967, 1969, 1970, 1972, 1988, 1994, 1995, 2011, 2014

Queen's University Belfast (8): 1959, 1965, 1971, 1982, 1990, 1993, 2000, 2007

University of Ulster, Jordanstown (UUJ), Antrim (5): 1986, 1987, 1991, 2001, 2008

Institute of Technology, Sligo (ITS) (3): 2002, 2004, 2005

Institute of Technology, Tralee (ITT), Kerry (3): 1997, 1998, 1999

Dublin City University (3): 2006, 2010, 2012

Cork Institute of Technology (1): 2009

St Mary's University College, Belfast (1): 1989

National University of Ireland, Maynooth (as St Patrick's College), Kildare (1): 1976

Dublin Institute of Technology (1): 2013

* not contested in 1921 and 1943

FITZGIBBON CUP

– The cup is named after Dr Edwin Fitzgibbon, a Capuchin friar who was also a professor of philosophy at University College Cork from 1911 to 1936.

- In 1912 Dr Fitzgibbon donated most of his annual salary to purchase the trophy. The cup was made at William Egan and Sons' silversmiths, Cork, and bears a large inscription including the date 'Feb. 1912' on its front.

- The cup is a 24-inch-tall silver trophy, with engraved Celtic designs. Its lid was lost in 1973 and never replaced.

- The competition was played on a round-robin basis until 1949, when a knockout format was adopted instead.

- UCC and UCD dominated the competition for the first thirty years.

- In 1933 UCC was awarded custody of the cup, but was not declared the formal winner, after a row over the eligibility of three players on the UCD winning team.

- Queen's University Belfast first took part in 1946 and won their only title in 1953.

- Nicky English, former Tipperary great, won five Fitzgibbon Cup medals in successive years with UCC, from 1981–85.

- In 1989 NIHE Limerick (now the University of Limerick) became the first non-university Fitzgibbon Cup champions.

– The first local derby final took place between Limerick Institute of Technology and the University of Limerick at the Gaelic Grounds, Limerick, in March 2005.

– The 2011–12 final, the first-ever all-Cork final, was staged at the newly refurbished Mardyke in the centenary year. Seamus Corry shot a late winner for UCC in extra time to beat CIT by 2–15 to 2–14.

– The 2007–08 final between Waterford IT and Limerick IT was the highest-scoring game in the competition's history. Joe Canning scored an incredible 1–16 for LIT, but still ended up on the losing side.

Roll of Honour*

University College Cork (41): 1913, 1918, 1920, 1922, 1924, 1925, 1928, 1929, 1930, 1931, 1933, 1937, 1939, 1947, 1955, 1956, 1957, 1959, 1962, 1963, 1966, 1967, 1971, 1972, 1976, 1981, 1982, 1983, 1984, 1985, 1986, 1987, 1988, 1990, 1991, 1996, 1997, 1998, 2009, 2012, 2013

University College Dublin (30): 1912, 1914, 1915, 1916, 1917, 1923, 1927, 1932, 1934, 1935, 1936, 1938, 1941, 1944, 1948, 1950, 1951, 1952, 1958, 1960, 1961, 1964, 1965, 1968, 1969, 1975, 1978, 1979, 1993, 2001

National University of Ireland, Galway (formerly UCG) (10): 1919, 1926, 1942, 1945, 1946, 1949, 1970, 1977, 1980, 2010

Waterford IT (formerly Waterford RTC) (9): 1992, 1995, 1999, 2000, 2003, 2004, 2006, 2008, 2014

University of Limerick (formerly NIHE, Limerick) (4): 1989, 1994, 2002, 2011

National University of Ireland, Maynooth (formerly St Patrick's) (2): 1973, 1974

Limerick Institute of Technology (2): 2005, 2007

Queens University Belfast (1): 1953

* not contested in 1921 and 1943, 1954 declared null and void

Fitzgibbon Cup, Winning Captains and Teams

1911–12: Edmond J. Ryan, UCD

1912–13: Peter M. Murphy, UCC

1913–14: Jim Reidy, UCC

1914–15: Éamon Bulfin, UCD

1915–16: John Ryan, UCD

1916–17: John Ryan, UCD

1917–18: Con Lucey, UCC

1918–19: Martin Fahy, UCG

1919–20: John R. Lahiffe, UCC

1920–21: Not Played

1921–22: Not Available, UCC

1922–23: Tommy Daly, UCD

1923–24: Tommy Daly, UCD

1924–25: Tom Lee, UCC

1925–26: Terence O'Grady, UCG

1926–27: Owen O'Neill, UCD

1927–28: Richard Molloy, UCC

1928–29: Paddy O'Donovan, UCC

1929–30: Patrick O'Donnell, UCC

1930–31: William Finlay, UCC

1931–32: Jack Walsh, UCD

1932–33: Richard Cronin, UCC

1933–34: Séamus Hogan, UCD

1934–35: Tom Loughnane, UCD

1935–36: Tony Mac Sullivan, UCD

1936–37: Mossie Roche, UCC

1937–38: Jimmy Cooney, UCD

1938–39: Jackie Spencer, UCC

1939–40: Jim Young, UCC (cup not awarded)

1940–41: Billy O'Neill, UCC

1941–42: Pat Hehir, UCG

1942–43: Not played

1943–44: Dick Stokes, UCD

1944–45: Michael Doyle, UCG

1945–46: Michael Doyle, UCG

1946–47: Mick Herlihy, UCC

1947–48: Frank Commons, UCD

1948–49: Johnny Scanlon, UCG

1949–50: Mick Maher, UCD

1950–51: Martin Fitzgerald, UCD

1951–52: Des Dillon, UCD

1952–53: Ted McConnell, QUB

1953–54: Pádraig 'Paddy' O'Donoghue, UCG (declared null & void)

1954–55: Pat Teehan, UCD

1956–57: Tony Murphy, UCC

1957–58: Bernard Hoey, UCD

1958–59: Steve Long, UCC

1959–60: Donie Nealon, UCD

1960–61: Owen O'Neill, UCD

1961–62: Jimmy Byrne, UCC

1962–63: Des Kiely, UCC

1963–64: Seán Quinlivan, UCD

1964–65: Murt Duggan, UCD

1965–66: Willie Cronin, UCC

1966–67: Seánie Barry, UCC

1967–68: Jim Furlong, UCD

1968–69: Pat Kavanagh, UCD

1969–70: Séamus Hogan, UCG

1970–71: Pat McDonnell, UCC

1971–72: Mick McCarthy, UCC

1972–73: Paudie Fitzmaurice, St Patrick's College Maynooth

1973–74: Paddy Barry, St Patrick's College Maynooth

1974–75: Séamus Ryan, UCD

1975–76: Donal McGovern, UCC

1976–77: Pat Fleury, UCG

1977–78: John Martin, UCD

1978–79: Tom Breen, UCD

1979–80: Vincent Daly, UCG

1980–81: John Minogue, UCC

1981–82: John Farrell, UCC

1982–83: Tadhg Coakley, UCC

1983–84: Mick Boylan, UCC

1984–85: Nicholas English, UCC

1985–86: Paul O'Connor, UCC

1986–87: John Grainger, UCC

1987–88: Andy O'Callaghan, UCC

1988–89: Dan Treacy, NIHE Limerick

1989–90: Mick Crowe, UCC

1990–91: Pat Heffernan, UCC

1991–92: Pádraic Fanning, Waterford RTC

1992–93: Jim Byrne, UCD

1993–94: Daragh O'Neill, UL

1994–95: Colm Bonnar, Waterford RTC

1995–96: Frank Lohan, UCC

1996–97: Kieran Morrison, UCC

1997–98: Eddie Enright, UCC

1998–99: Andy Moloney, Waterford IT

1999–00: Andy Moloney, Waterford IT

2000–01: David Hegarty, UCD

2001–02: Eoin Fitzgerald, UL

2002–03: Paul Curran, Waterford IT

2003–04: J. J. Delaney, Waterford IT

2004–05: Eoin Kelly, Limerick IT

2005–06: Brian Dowling, Waterford IT and Hugh Maloney, Waterford IT (joint captains)

2006–07: Kieran Murphy, Limerick IT

2007–08: Kevin Moran, Waterford IT

2008–09: Kevin Hartnett, UCC

2009–10: Finian Coone, NUI Galway

2010–11: Kieran Joyce, UL

2011–12: Shane Bourke, UCC

2012–13: Darren McCarthy, UCC

2013–14: Eoin Murphy, Waterford IT

THE DR HARTY CUP, MUNSTER HURLING, SENIOR COLLEGES A

-   The Dr Harty Cup is the premier hurling competition for schools in the province of Munster.

-   St Flannan's are the most successful team in the competition's history, notching up twenty-one victories.

-   Rockwell College won the first competition in 1918.

-   Players have to be under the age of eighteen and a half to compete. The winning team represents the province in the Dr Croke Cup.

-   In the past few years, the runner-up also enters the All-Ireland colleges competition (Croke Cup).

-   The 2009 final was won by Thurles CBS, who won their first title since 1956.

-   There will be no defending champions in the 2014 Dr Harty Cup. Dungarvan Colleges, composed of Dungarvan CBS and St Augustine's, won a second consecutive title in 2013, but no amalgamated sides are in this year's competition.

Roll of Honour*

St Flannan's, Ennis (21): 1944, 1945, 1946, 1947, 1952, 1954, 1957, 1958, 1976, 1979, 1982, 1983, 1987, 1989, 1990, 1991, 1998, 1999, 2000, 2004, 2005

North Monastery, Cork (19): 1919, 1929, 1934, 1935,

1936, 1937, 1940, 1941, 1942, 1943, 1955, 1960, 1961, 1970, 1980, 1981, 1985, 1986, 1994

Limerick CBS (10): 1920, 1925, 1926, 1927, 1932, 1964, 1965, 1966, 1967, 1993

St Colman's College, Fermoy (9): 1948, 1949, 1977, 1992, 1996, 1997, 2001, 2002, 2003

Thurles CBS (7): 1933, 1938, 1939, 1950, 1951, 1956, 2009

St Finbarr's, Cork (7): 1963, 1969, 1971, 1972, 1973, 1974, 1984

Rockwell College (5): 1918, 1923, 1924, 1930, 1931

Midleton CBS (3): 1988, 1995, 2006

Ardscoil Rís, Limerick (3): 2010, 2011, 2014

De La Salle College, Waterford (2): 2007, 2008

Colaiste na nDeise/Dungarvan Colleges (2): 2012, 2013

St Munchin's (2): 1921, 1922

Mount Sion (1): 1953

Abbey CBS, Tipperary town (1): 1959

Rice College, Ennis (1): 1962

Coláiste Chríost Rí (1): 1968

Colaiste Iognaid Ris, Cork (1): 1975

Templemore CBS (1): 1978

* not contested in 1928

CROKE CUP, ALL-IRELAND HURLING, SENIOR COLLEGES A

– The Croke Cup is presented to the winner of the

All-Ireland Senior Colleges 'A' hurling championship.

- The cup is called after the famous Bishop Croke, in whose honour Croke Park is also named.

- The cup was formerly used for an inter-county GAA competition in hurling.

- The first inter-county Croke Cups (which included hurling and football) took place between 1896 and 1915.

- Clare was the first winner of the inter-county Croke Cup for hurling in 1896.

- St Flannan's of Ennis were the first winners of the Croke cup in its current incarnation as the All-Ireland senior colleges competition in 1944.

- St Kieran's of Kilkenny are the most dominant team in the competition's history. They have also won a record fifty-two Leinster Senior College titles.

- Kilkenny greats Henry Shefflin and Eddie Keher represented St Kieran's College, as did former Wexford star Nicky Rackard and Tipperary's Eoin Kelly.

Roll of Honour*

St Kieran's, Kilkenny (19): 1948, 1957, 1959, 1961, 1965, 1971, 1975, 1988, 1989, 1990, 1992, 1993, 1996, 2000, 2003, 2004, 2010, 2011, 2014

St Flannan's, Ennis (14): 1944, 1945, 1946, 1947, 1958, 1976, 1979, 1982, 1983, 1987, 1991, 1998, 1999, 2005

North Monastery, Cork (5): 1960, 1970, 1980, 1985, 1994

St Finbarr's, Cork (5): 1963, 1969, 1972, 1974, 1984

St Peter's College, Wexford (4): 1962, 1967, 1968, 1973

St Colman's College, Fermoy (4): 1977, 1997, 2001, 2002

Limerick CBS (2): 1964, 1966

De La Salle College, Waterford (2): 2007, 2008

Templemore CBS (1): 1978

Kilkenny CBS (1): 1981

Birr Community School, Offaly (1): 1986

St Raphael's, Loughrea (1): 1995

Dublin Colleges (1): 2006

Thurles CBS (1): 2009

Nenagh CBS (1): 2012

Dungarvan Colleges (1): 2013

* not contested in 1949–56

HOGAN CUP, ALL-IRELAND COLLEGES SENIOR FOOTBALL

- The Hogan Cup (Irish: Corn Uí Ógáin) is presented to the winners of the All-Ireland Senior Colleges 'A' football championship.

- St Jarlath's College, Tuam, hold the record number of titles, winning their twelfth in 2002.

- St Jarlath's have also been runners-up in a further fourteen finals.

- Second overall on the roll of honour, are eight-times champions St Colman's, Newry, who in 2011 retained the title for the first time in their history with victory over St Jarlath's College.

- Inaugurated in 1946, this trophy is named after Brother Thomas Hogan. (The Hogan Stand in Croke Park is named after his brother Michael.)

Roll of Honour*

St Jarlath's College, Tuam (12): 1947, 1958, 1960, 1961, 1964, 1966, 1974, 1978, 1982, 1984, 1994, 2002

St Colman's, Newry (8): 1967, 1975, 1986, 1988, 1993, 1998, 2010, 2011

St Patrick's College, Maghera (5): 1989, 1990, 1995, 2003, 2013

St Mel's, Longford (4): 1948, 1962, 1963, 1987

Coláiste Chríost Rí, Cork (4): 1968, 1970, 1983, 1985

Carmelite College, Moate (3): 1976, 1980, 1981

St Patrick's, Navan (3): 2000, 2001, 2004

St Brendan's, Killarney (2): 1969, 1992

St Patrick's Academy, Dungannon (2): 1997, 2008

St Patrick's Grammar School, Armagh (1): 1946

St Nathy's, Ballaghaderreen (1): 1957

St Joseph's, Fairview (1): 1959

St Columb's, Derry (1): 1965

St Mary's CBS, Belfast (1): 1971

St Patrick's, Cavan (1): 1972

Franciscan College, Gormanstown (1): 1973

St Colman's College, Claremorris (1): 1977

Ardscoil Rís, Dublin (1): 1979

St Fachtna's, Skibbereen (1): 1991

Intermediate School, Killorglin (1): 1996

Good Counsel, New Ross (1): 1999

Knockbeg College, Carlow (1): 2005

Abbey CBS, Newry (1): 2006

Omagh CBS (1): 2007

Colaiste Na Sceilge, Caherciveen (1): 2009

St Mary's, Edenderry (1): 2012

Pobalscoil Chorca Dhuibhne, Dingle (1): 2014

* not contested in 1949–56

VOCATIONAL SCHOOLS SENIOR FOOTBALL

–   The competition was launched in 1975.

–   Tralee won the first final defeating Virginia Vocational school.

–   Newry dominated the early years, winning six of the first nine competitions.

–   Colaiste Na Sceilge, Caherciveen, are the only school to have won the two All-Ireland senior 'A' secondary school competitions, the Vocational Schools 'A' championship (2000) and the Hogan Cup (2009).

–   Newry are the only side to have won three-in-a-row (1980–82).

Roll of Honour

Newry (6): 1976, 1977, 1981, 1982, 1983, 1986

Tralee (3): 1975, 1980, 1991

Rathmore Post Primary (2): 1978, 1995

Dungannon HS (2): 1989, 1990

Holy Trinity College, Cookstown (2): 1998, 2012

Caherciveen PPS (2): 1999, 2000

St Ciaran's HS, Ballygawley (2): 2002, 2005

Virginia VS (2): 2006, 2007

St Malachy's, Castlewellan (2): 2008, 2009

St Pius X, Magherafelt (1): 1979

Armagh Technical College (1): 1984

Edenderry (1): 1985

Rathmore CC, Kerry (1): 1987

Colaiste Gobnait, Cork (1): 1988

Tullow Community School (1): 1992

Rathmore CS (1): 1993

Beara CS, Cork (1): 1994

Fermanagh CFE (1): 1996

Scoil Ui Chonaill, Caherciveen (1): 1997

Ard Scoil Chiaráin, Offaly (1): 2001

Causeway Comprehensive, Kerry (1): 2003

St Brogan's, Bandon (1): 2004

Clonakilty CC (1): 2010

Gallen CS, Ferbane (1): 2011

Cnoc Mhuire, Granard (1): 2013

VOCATIONAL SCHOOLS SENIOR HURLING

- The competition was launched in 1978.

- St Brigid's are the most successful team in Vocational Schools Senior Hurling with nine titles.

- When Roscrea won in 1980 they had a famous teacher in charge. Seamus Dennison, who was an Irish rugby international and a member of the Munster team that defeated the All Blacks, was at the helm.

- Gort won the first final with a score of 5–5 to Enniscorthy's 3–5.

- St Brogan's of Bandon are the only team to have won both Senior Vocational titles. They won both the hurling and football competitions in 2004.

- Johnstown became the first Kilkenny side to win the All-Ireland individual senior schools title when they triumphed in 1982.

Roll of Honour*

St Brigid's, Loughrea (9): 1995, 1996, 2000, 2001, 2002, 2003, 2007, 2009, 2011

Athenry, Galway (5): 1992, 1993, 1994, 1998, 1999

Banagher College, Offaly (4): 1985, 1986, 1989, 2010

Roscrea, Tipperary (2): 1980, 1991

Colaiste Mhuire, Johnstown (2): 1982, 2008

Moneenageisha, Galway (2): 1988, 1990

St Fergal's, Rathdowney (2): 2006, 2013

Gort, Galway (1): 1978

Ennis (1): 1979

New Inn, Galway (1): 1981

Portumna, Galway (1): 1983

Nenagh, Tipperary (1): 1984

Thomastown, Kilkenny (1): 1987

Mannix College, Rathluirc (1): 1997

St Brogan's, Bandon (1): 2004

Borrisokane, Tipperary (1): 2005

* not contested in 2012

POC FADA

- The All-Ireland Poc Fada Hurling & Camogie Championships is an annual skills competition featuring some of Ireland's best hurlers and camogie players. The Irish term Poc Fada translates as 'long puck'.

- The championships are currently sponsored by Today FM and M. Donnelly & Co. (since 1996), owned by Clare businessman and GAA fan Michael Donnelly.

- Since 2005 the All-Ireland Poc Fada finals have taken place on the Saturday of the Irish August Bank Holiday each year.

- The starting time is 11.30 a.m. On the shorter course (2.5 km) the Boys Under-16 final begins first, followed by the Camogie final, with the Senior final following on the 5 km course.

- The Senior Hurling final starts at Annaverna, County Louth in the Cooley Peninsula. Competitors must puck a sliotar with a hurley to the top of Annaverna Mountain, then onward to Carnavaddy Hill. Then, after an interval, they continue down to An Gabhlán Hill, before reaching the finishing line at An Fhána Mór, Annaverna. The total course length measures 5 km (3.1 miles).

- Brendan Cummins of Tipperary holds the course

record at forty-eight pucks, the lowest amount of strokes ever taken to complete the competition.

- 2013 All-Ireland-winning manager Davy Fitzgerald (Clare) won in 1999, at the ninth time of trying.

- Patricia Jackman from Waterford has won the camogie competition five times.

POC FADA NATIONAL COMPETITIONS

Senior Final – An Corn Setanta (Setanta Cup)

The twelve competitors competing in this category are the four provincial champions, the provincial runners-up, the current champion, the 2013 'All-Star' goalkeeper and two invitationals (which can feature competitors from all over the world including the USA, Europe and South Africa). An Corn Setanta is awarded to the player who takes the lowest amount of pucks to finish the course. In the event of a tie, the distance by which the player's last puck crosses the finish line will determine the winner.

Camogie Final – The Camogie Poc Fada Cup

There are seven competitors in the ladies event, but if there is an invitational place/wildcard competitor this rises to eight. The line-up includes the current champion, the winners from the four provinces, a qualifier from Co. Louth and a qualifier from Co. Armagh (the latter two counties being the hosts). In the past the invitational/wildcard has gone to the London Cumann.

The Under-16 Boys Final – The Sean Óg Mac Seáin Cup

There are currently only four contestants in the competition, one from each of the four provincial qualifiers. If the winner of the All-Ireland final is eligible to compete in the same age group the following year, he will be invited to return and defend his All-Ireland title. To date this has happened on only one occasion, when the 2011 Under-16 champion, Cillian Kiely of Offaly, successfully retained the All-Ireland title in 2012.

HISTORY

– The idea for the competition came from the 'Táin Bó Cuailgne', the legendary tale of Cúchulainn. As a boy he set out from his home at Dún Dealgan for the king's court at Emain Macha, hitting the sliotar before him and running ahead to catch it.

– The tournament was founded in 1960 by Fr Pól Mac Sheáin and the Naomh Moninne club in Fatima, Dundalk, Co. Louth.

– The inaugural All-Ireland competition took place in 1961. Limerick man Vincent Godfrey became the first winner out of a field of sixteen hurlers.

– The competition was not held between 1969 and 1980. It returned in 1981, this time with twelve competitors.

– In 2001 the competition had to be held at Dundalk

Racecourse because of an outbreak of foot-and-mouth disease on the Cooley Peninsula.

– In the 2005 tournament Irish international soccer player Niall Quinn (who played for Dublin in the All-Ireland minor final of 1983) took part as an invited entrant. It was won by Albert Shanahan of Limerick.

– Almost all of the winners of both the men's and women's competition have been from the traditional hurling counties, with a few exceptions: Dinny Donnelly (Meath), Gerry Goodwin (Tyrone), Colin Byrne (Wicklow), Paul Dunne (Louth), Mary Henry (Westmeath), Gerry Fallon (Roscommon) and Graham Clarke (Down).

– Goalkeepers have a rich tradition of winning the tournament. An early winner was Kilkenny net minder Ollie Walsh. The 1980s were dominated by former Cork net minder Ger Cunningham, who won seven in a row. Davy Fitzgerald of Clare won in 1999 and 2002, and in recent years Brendan Cummins of Tipperary has reigned supreme as 'King of the Mountains'.

– Brendan Cummins' course record of forty-eight pucks works out at an average of 104 metres per puck.

– The camogie course record was set in 2008, by Lyndsey Condell of Carlow (twenty-eight pucks and 67 metres over the end line).

ROLL OF HONOUR, SENIOR COMPETITION

1961: Vincent Godfrey, Limerick

1962: Ollie Walsh, Kilkenny

1963: Tom Geary, Waterford; Dinny Donnelly, Meath; Ollie Walsh, Kilkenny (all tied)

1964: Oliver Gough, Kilkenny

1965: Denis Murphy, Cork

1966–68: Finbar O'Neill, Cork

1969: Liam Tobin, Waterford

1970–80: No competition

1981: Pat Hartigan, Limerick

1982: Gerry Goodwin, Tyrone

1983: Pat Hartigan, Limerick

1984–90: Ger Cunningham, Cork

1991: Tommy Quaid, Limerick

1992–93: Albert Kelly, Offaly

1994–96: Michael Shaughnessy, Galway

1997: Colin Byrne, Wicklow

1998: Albert Kelly, Offaly

1999: Davy Fitzgerald, Clare

2000: Colin Byrne, Wicklow

2001: Albert Shanahan, Limerick

2002: Davy Fitzgerald, Clare

2003: Paul Dunne, Louth

2004: Brendan Cummins, Tipperary

2005: Albert Shanahan, Limerick

2006–08: Brendan Cummins, Tipperary

2009: Gerry Fallon, Roscommon

2010: Graham Clarke, Down

2011–13: Brendan Cummins, Tipperary

COUNTIES FROM A TO Z

ANTRIM

Irish: Aontroim
Province: Ulster
Nicknames: The Saffrons, The Glensmen
County colours: Saffron and white
Competitions: NFL: Division 4; NHL: Division 1B
Football Championship: Sam Maguire Cup
Hurling Championship: Liam MacCarthy Cup
Ladies' Gaelic football: Brendan Martin Cup
Camogie: Jack McGrath Cup
Ground: Casement Park (Páirc Mhic Easmainn)
Location: Belfast
Renovated: 2000; 2013–15 (in progress)
Capacity: 32,600
Field dimensions: 145 x 90m

ARMAGH

Irish: Ard Mhacha
Province: Ulster
Nickname: The Orchard County
County colours: Orange and white
Competitions: NFL: Division 3; NHL: Division 2B
Football Championship: Sam Maguire Cup
Hurling Championship: Christy Ring Cup

Ladies' Gaelic football: Brendan Martin Cup

Camogie: Nancy Murray Cup

Ground: Athletic Grounds (Páirc Lúthchleasaíochta)

Location: Armagh town, Co. Armagh

Opened: 1920s

Renovated: 2011

Capacity: 16,500

Field dimensions: 143 x 88m

CARLOW

Irish: Ceatharlach

Province: Leinster

Nickname: The Scallion Eaters

County colours: Red, green and gold

Competitions: NFL: Division 4; NHL: Division 2A

Football Championship: Sam Maguire Cup

Hurling Championship: Liam MacCarthy Cup

Ladies' Gaelic football: Brendan Martin Cup

Camogie: Nancy Murray Cup

Ground: Dr Cullen Park (Páirc Uí Chuilinn)

Location: Carlow town, Co. Carlow

Renovated: 2003

Capacity: 21,000

Field dimensions: 145 x 87m

CAVAN

Irish: An Cabhán

Province: Ulster
Nickname: The Breffni Men
County colours: Blue and white
Competitions: NFL: Division 3; NHL: n/a
Football Championship: Sam Maguire Cup
Hurling Championship: Lory Meagher Cup
Ladies' Gaelic football: Brendan Martin Cup
Camogie: Nancy Murray Cup
Ground: Kingspan Breffni Park (Páirc Bhreifne)
Location: Cavan town, Co. Cavan
Opened: 1923
Capacity: 32,000
Field dimensions: 143 x 86m

CLARE

Irish: An Clár
Province: Munster
Nickname: The Banner County
County colours: Saffron and blue
Competitions: NFL: Division 3; NHL: Division 1A
Football Championship: Sam Maguire Cup
Hurling Championship: Liam MacCarthy Cup
Ladies' Gaelic football: Brendan Martin Cup
Camogie: O'Duffy Cup
Ground: Cusack Park (Páirc Uí Chíosóg)
Location: Ennis, Co. Clare
Renovated: 2009

Capacity: 14,864
Field dimensions: 145 x 90m

CORK
Irish: Corcaigh
Province: Munster
Nickname: The Rebels
County colours: Red and white
Competitions: NFL: Division 1; NHL: Division 1
Football Championship: Sam Maguire Cup
Hurling Championship: Liam MacCarthy Cup
Ladies' Gaelic Football: Brendan Martin Cup
Camogie: O'Duffy Cup
Main Ground: Páirc Uí Chaoimh
Location: Blackrock, Cork city
Opened: 1976
Renovated: 2008
Capacity: 43,550
Field dimensions: 144 x 88m
Other Ground: Páirc Uí Rinn
Opened: 23 May 1993
Location: Cork city
Capacity: 16,440
Field dimensions: 144 x 88m

DERRY
Irish: Doire
Province: Ulster

Nickname: The Oak Leaf County

County colours: Red and white

Competitions: NFL: Division 1; NHL: Division 2A

Football Championship: Sam Maguire Cup

Hurling Championship: Christy Ring Cup

Ladies' Gaelic football: Brendan Martin Cup

Camogie: Jack McGrath Cup

Ground: Celtic Park (Páirc na gCeilteach)

Location: Derry city

Renovated: 2009

Capacity: 22,000

Field dimensions: 138 x 84m

DONEGAL

Irish: Dún na nGall

Province: Ulster

Nickname: The Tir Conaill Men

County colours: Gold and green

Competitions: NFL: Division 1; NHL: Division 2B

Football Championship: Sam Maguire Cup

Hurling Championship: Christy Ring Cup

Ladies' Gaelic football: Brendan Martin Cup

Camogie: O'Duffy Cup

Ground: MacCumhail Park (Páirc Sheáin Mac Cumhaill)

Location: Ballybofey, Co. Donegal

Capacity: 18,000

Field dimensions: 145 x 90m

DOWN

Irish: An Dún

Province: Ulster

Nicknames: The Mournemen (football), The Ardsmen (hurling)

County colours: Red and black

Competitions: NFL: Division 2; NHL: Division 2B

Football Championship: Sam Maguire Cup

Hurling Championship: Christy Ring Cup

Ladies' Gaelic football: Brendan Martin Cup

Camogie: Kay Mills Cup

Ground: Páirc Esler (formerly Páirc an Iúir)

Location: Newry, Co. Down

Renovated: 2006–07

Capacity: 20,000

Field dimensions: 138 x 81m

DUBLIN

Irish: Áth Cliath

Province: Leinster

Nicknames: The Dubs, The Jacks, The Boys in Blue

County colours: Sky and navy blue

Competitions: NFL: Division 1; NHL: Division 1A

Football Championship: Sam Maguire Cup

Hurling Championship: Liam MacCarthy Cup

Ladies' Gaelic football: Brendan Martin Cup

Camogie: O'Duffy Cup

Main Ground: Croke Park (Páirc an Chrócaigh)

Location: Dublin 3

Opened: 1913

Renovated: 2004 (cost: €260 million)

Capacity: 82,300

Field dimensions: 144.5 x 88m

Other Ground: Parnell Park

Location: Donnycarney, Dublin

Capacity: 13,499

Field dimensions: 141 x 82m

FERMANAGH

Irish: Fear Manach

Province: Ulster

Nickname: The Ernesiders

County colours: Green and white

Competitions: NFL: Division 3; NHL: Division 3A

Football Championship: Sam Maguire Cup

Hurling Championship: Lory Meagher Cup

Ladies' Gaelic football: Brendan Martin Cup

Camogie: Do not compete

Ground: Brewster Park (Páirc an Bruiscear)

Location: Enniskillen, Co. Fermanagh

Renovated: 2007

Capacity: 18,000

Field dimensions: 145 x 83m

FINGAL (DUBLIN) GAA

Irish: Fine Gall

Nicknames: The Ravens, The Northsiders

County colours: Purple and white

Competition: NHL: Division 3A

Hurling Championship: Nicky Rackard Cup

Ground: Lawless Memorial Park

Location: Swords, Co. Dublin

GALWAY

Irish: Gaillimh

Province: Connacht

Nickname: The Tribesmen

County colours: Maroon and white

Competitions: NFL: Division 2; NHL: Division 1A

Football Championship: Sam Maguire Cup

Hurling Championship: Liam MacCarthy Cup

Ladies' Gaelic football: Brendan Martin Cup

Camogie: O'Duffy Cup

Ground: Pearse Stadium (Páirc an Phiarsaigh)

Location: Dr Mannix Road, Salthill

Opened: 1957 (construction cost: IR£34,000)

Renovated: 2003

Capacity: 26,197

Field dimensions: 145 x 90m

KERRY

Irish: Ciarraí

Province: Munster

Nickname: The Kingdom

County colours: Green and gold

Competitions: NFL: Division 1; NHL: Division 2A

Football Championship: Sam Maguire Cup

Hurling Championship: Christy Ring Cup

Ladies' Gaelic football: Brendan Martin Cup

Camogie: Do not compete

Main Ground: Fitzgerald Stadium (Staidiam Mhic Gearailt)

Location: Killarney, Co. Kerry

Opened: 1936

Renovated: 2009

Capacity: 43,180 (9,000 seated)

Field dimensions: 144 x 82m

Other Ground: Austin Stack Park (Páirc Aibhistin De Staic)

Location: Tralee, Co. Kerry

Renovated: 2007

Capacity: 18,000

KILDARE

Irish: Cill Dara

Province: Leinster

Nickname: The Lilywhites

County colours: All white

Competitions: NFL: Division 2; NHL: Division 2B

Football Championship: Sam Maguire Cup
Hurling Championship: Christy Ring Cup
Ladies' Gaelic football: Brendan Martin Cup
Camogie: Kay Mills Cup
Ground: St Conleth's Park (Páirc Naoimh Conlaith)
Location: Newbridge, Co. Kildare
Capacity: 6,200
Field dimensions: 135 x 80m

KILKENNY
Irish: Cill Chainnigh
Province: Leinster
Nickname: The Cats
County colours: Black and amber
Competitions: NFL: n/a; NHL: Division 1A
Football Championship: Junior Football Championship
Hurling Championship: Liam MacCarthy Cup
Ladies' Gaelic football: Brendan Martin Cup
Camogie: O'Duffy Cup
Ground: Nowlan Park
Location: Kilkenny city, Co. Kilkenny
Capacity: 24,000
Field dimensions: 145 x 88m

LAOIS
Irish: Laois
Province: Leinster
Nickname: The O'Moore County

County colours: Blue and white
Competitions: NFL: Division 2; NHL: Division 1B
Football Championship: Sam Maguire Cup
Hurling Championship: Liam MacCarthy Cup
Camogie: Kay Mills Cup
Ground: O'Moore Park (Páirc Uí Mhórdha)
Location: Portlaoise, Co. Laois
Renovated: 2002
Capacity: 27,000
Field dimensions: 142 x 86m

LEITRIM

Irish: Liatroim
Province: Connacht
Nickname: The Ridge County
County colours: Gold and green
Competitions: NFL: Division 4; NHL: Division 3B
Football Championship: Sam Maguire Cup
Hurling Championship: Lory Meagher Cup
Ladies' Gaelic football: Mary Quinn Memorial Cup
Camogie: Do not compete
Ground: Páirc Seán Mac Diarmada
Location: Carrick-on-Shannon, Co. Leitrim
Renovated: 2007
Capacity: 9,331
Field dimensions: 142 x 87m

LIMERICK

Irish: Luimneach

Province: Munster

Nicknames: The Shannonsiders, The Treaty County

County colours: Green and white

Competitions: NFL: Division 3; NHL: Division 1B

Football Championship: Sam Maguire Cup

Hurling Championship: Liam MacCarthy Cup

Ladies' Gaelic football: Brendan Martin Cup

Camogie: Jack McGrath Cup

Ground: Gaelic Grounds (Páirc na nGael)

Location: Limerick city

Renovated: 2004

Capacity: 49,866

Field dimensions: 137 x 82m

LONDON

Irish: Londain

Nickname: The Exiles

County colours: Green and white

Competitions: NFL: Division 4; NHL: Division 2A

Football Championship: Sam Maguire Cup

Hurling Championship: Liam MacCarthy Cup

Ladies' Gaelic football: Brendan Martin Cup

Camogie: Máire Ní Chinnéide Cup

Ground: Emerald GAA Grounds (Páirc Smáirgaid)

Location: South Ruislip, London

LONGFORD

Irish: An Longfort

Province: Leinster

Nickname: The Slashers

County colours: Royal blue and gold

Competitions: NFL: Division 4; NHL: Division 3B

Football Championship: Sam Maguire Cup

Hurling Championship: Lory Meagher Cup

Ladies' Gaelic football: Brendan Martin Cup

Camogie: Do not compete

Ground: Pearse Park (Páirc an Phiarsaigh)

Location: Longford, Co. Longford

Capacity: 10,000

Field dimensions: 138 x 88m

LOUTH

Irish: Lughbhadh or An Lú

Province: Leinster

Nickname: The Wee County

County colours: Red and white

Competitions: NFL: Division 3; NHL: Division 3A

Football Championship: Sam Maguire Cup

Hurling Championship: Nicky Rackard Cup

Camogie: Do not compete

Ground: Drogheda Park (Páirc Dhroichead Átha)

Location: Drogheda, Co. Louth

Capacity: 3,500

Field dimensions: 138 x 83m

MAYO

Irish: Maigh Eo
Province: Connacht
Nickname: None
County colours: Green and red
Competitions: NFL: Division 1; NHL: Division 2B
Football Championship: Sam Maguire Cup
Hurling Championship: Christy Ring Cup
Ladies' Gaelic football: Brendan Martin Cup
Camogie: Do not compete
Ground: McHale Park (Páirc Mhic Éil)
Location: Castlebar, Co. Mayo
Opened: 1931
Capacity: 36,000
Field dimensions: 137 x 82m

MEATH

Irish: An Mhí
Province: Leinster
Nickname: The Royals
County colours: Green and gold
Competitions: NFL: Division 2; NHL: Division 2B
Football Championship: Sam Maguire Cup
Hurling Championship: Christy Ring Cup
Ladies' Gaelic football: Brendan Martin Cup
Camogie: Kay Mills Cup
Ground: Tailteann Park (Páirc Tailteann)
Location: Navan, Co. Meath

Opened: 1935
Capacity: 10,000
Field dimensions: 135 x 87m

MONAGHAN
Irish: Muineachán
Province: Ulster
Nickname: The Farney County
County colours: White with blue trim
Competitions: NFL: Division 1; NHL: Division 3A
Football Championship: Sam Maguire Cup
Hurling Championship: Nicky Rackard Cup
Ladies' Gaelic football: Brendan Martin Cup
Camogie: Máire Ní Chinnéide Cup
Ground: St Tiernach's Park (Páirc Thiarnaigh Naofa)
Location: Clones, Co. Monaghan
Opened: 1944
Renovated: 1992–93 (cost: IR£4.5 million)
Capacity: 36,000
Field dimensions: 142 x 87m

NEW YORK
Irish: Nua Eabhrac
Nickname: The Exiles
County colours: Red, white and blue
Football Championship: Sam Maguire Cup
Ground: The Gaelic Park Sports Centre (Páirc na nGael)
Location: The Bronx, New York city

Opened: 1926
Renovated: 2007 (cost: $3 million)
Capacity: 2,000

OFFALY

Irish: Uíbh Fhailí
Province: Leinster
Nickname: The Faithful County
County colours: White, green and gold
Competitions: NFL: Division 4; NHL: Division 1B
Football Championship: Sam Maguire Cup
Hurling Championship: Liam MacCarthy Cup
Ground: O'Connor Park (Páirc Uí Conaire)
Location: Tullamore, Co. Offaly
Opened: 1934
Renovated: 2004–06
Capacity: 20,000
Field dimensions: 145 x 90m

ROSCOMMON

Irish: Ros Comáin
Province: Connacht
Nicknames: The Rossies, Sheep Stealers
County colours: Primrose and blue (black and green until 1935)
Competitions: NFL: Division 2; NHL: Division 3A
Football Championship: Sam Maguire Cup

Hurling Championship: Nicky Rackard Cup

Ladies' Gaelic football: Brendan Martin Cup

Camogie: Kay Mills Cup

Ground: Dr Hyde Park (Páirc de hÍde)

Location: Athlone Road, Roscommon town

Opened: 1969

Capacity: 18,500

Field dimensions: 145 x 90m

SLIGO

Irish: Sligeach

Province: Connacht

Nickname: The Yeats County

County colours: Black and white

Competitions: NFL: Division 3; NHL: Division 3B

Football Championship: Sam Maguire Cup

Hurling Championship: Nicky Rackard Cup

Ladies' Gaelic football: Brendan Martin Cup

Camogie: Do not compete

Ground: Markievicz Park (Páirc Markiewicz)

Location: Sligo town, Co. Sligo

Opened: 1955

Capacity: 18,558

Field dimensions: 142 x 90m

TIPPERARY

Irish: Tiobraid Árann

Province: Munster

Nickname: The Premier County

County colours: Blue and gold

Competitions: NFL: Division 4; NHL: Division 1A

Football Championship: Sam Maguire Cup

Hurling Championship: Liam MacCarthy Cup

Ladies' Gaelic football: Brendan Martin Cup

Camogie: O'Duffy Cup

Ground: Semple Stadium (Staid Semple)

Location: Thurles, Co. Tipperary

Opened: 1910

Renovated: 1981 and 2009

Capacity: 53,000

Field dimensions: 145 x 90m

TYRONE

Irish: Tír Eoghain

Province: Ulster

Nicknames: The O'Neill County, the Red Hands

County colours: White and red

Competitions: NFL: Division 1; NHL: Division 3A

Football Championship: Sam Maguire Cup

Hurling Championship: Nicky Rackard Cup

Ladies' Gaelic football: Brendan Martin Cup

Camogie: Nancy Murray Cup

Ground: Healy Park (Páirc Uí hÉilí)

Location: Omagh, Co. Tyrone

Opened: 1972

Renovated: 2001 (cost €2 million)
Capacity: 18,500
Field dimensions: 142 x 86m

WARWICKSHIRE
Nickname: Warks
County colours: White and black
Competitions: NHL: Division 3B
Hurling Championship: Lory Meagher Cup
Ground: Páirc na hÉireann
Location: Solihull, West Midlands, England

WATERFORD
Irish: Port Láirge
Province: Munster
Nickname: The Déise
County colours: White and blue
Competitions: NFL: Division 4; NHL: Division 1B
Football Championship: Sam Maguire Cup
Hurling Championship: Liam MacCarthy Cup
Ladies' Gaelic football: Brendan Martin Cup
Camogie: Kay Mills Cup
Main Ground: Fraher Field
Location: Dungarvan, Co. Waterford
Capacity: 15,000
Other Ground: Walsh Park
Capacity: 17,000
Field dimensions: 142 x 80m

WESTMEATH

Irish: An Iarmhí

Province: Leinster

Nickname: The Lake County

County colours: Maroon and white

Competitions: NFL: Division 2; NHL: Division 2A

Football Championship: Sam Maguire Cup

Hurling Championship: Liam MacCarthy Cup

Ladies' Gaelic football: Brendan Martin Cup

Camogie: Nancy Murray Cup

Ground: Cusack Park (Páirc Uí Chíosóg)

Location: Mullingar, Co. Westmeath

Opened: 1933

Capacity: 11,000

Field dimensions: 140 x 82m

WEXFORD

Irish: Loch Garman

Province: Leinster

Nicknames: The Model County, The Yellowbellies, The Slaneysiders

County colours: Purple and gold

Competitions: NFL: Division 3; NHL: Division 1B

Football Championship: Sam Maguire Cup

Hurling Championship: Liam MacCarthy Cup

Ladies' Gaelic football: Brendan Martin Cup

Camogie: O'Duffy Cup

Ground: Wexford Park (Páirc Loch Garman)

Location: Clonard, County Wexford

Capacity: 25,000

WICKLOW

Irish: Cill Mhantáin

Province: Leinster

Nickname: The Garden County

County colours: Blue and gold

Competitions: NFL: Division 4; NHL: Division 2A

Football Championship: Sam Maguire Cup

Hurling Championship: Christy Ring Cup

Ladies' Gaelic football: Brendan Martin Cup

Camogie: Máire Ní Chinnéide Cup

Ground: Aughrim County Ground

Location: Aughrim, County Wicklow

Capacity: 10,000

LADIES GAA

ALL-IRELAND CAMOGIE CHAMPIONSHIP

–   The All-Ireland Camogie final is played on the second Sunday in September in Croke Park, Dublin.

–   The first Camogie Association was founded in Dublin in 1904.

–   Dublin won the first All-Ireland camogie final (played in 1932) captained by Association President Máire Gill. They defeated Galway 3–2 to 0–2 at Galway Sportsfield.

–   The 1942 final was the first radio broadcast of the sport.

–   Angela Downey scored a famous goal in 1989, despite the fact she lost both hurley and skirt as she bore down on goal. Downey went on to become a camogie legend and won twelve All-Ireland medals.

–   Dublin have won the All-Ireland Senior Camogie Championship the most times – twenty-six titles as of 1984, the last time they won.

–   For a twenty-year period, from 1974 until 1994, the Kilkenny camogie team had a virtual monopoly on the championship.

–   Since 1997 Cork have emerged as one of the

dominant forces, winning seven All-Ireland titles, their latest in 2009.

- Despite their rich hurling tradition, Tipperary's first camogie title did not arrive until 1999. They duly made up for lost time, by winning three All-Irelands in a row.

- Between 1999 and 2006 Tipperary won five All-Ireland titles from eight consecutive final appearances.

- Six counties – Louth (1934 and 1936), Waterford (1945), Down (1948), Derry (1954), Mayo (1959) and Limerick (1980) – have appeared in All-Ireland finals without ever winning the O'Duffy Cup.

- Three counties – Kildare (1933), Cavan (1940 and 1941) and Clare (1944 and 1978) – have contested the penultimate semi-final stage without qualifying for a final.

- London have reached the All-Ireland final, in what were effectively play-offs between the All-Ireland champions and British provincial champions in 1949 and 1950.

Roll of Honour

Dublin (26): 1932, 1933, 1937, 1938, 1942, 1943, 1944, 1948, 1949, 1950, 1951, 1952, 1953, 1954, 1955, 1957, 1958, 1959, 1960, 1961, 1962, 1963, 1964, 1965, 1966, 1984

Cork (24): 1934, 1935, 1936, 1939, 1940, 1941, 1970,

1971, 1972, 1973, 1978, 1980, 1982, 1983, 1992, 1993, 1995, 1997, 1998, 2002, 2005, 2006, 2008, 2009

Kilkenny (12): 1974, 1976, 1977, 1981, 1985, 1986, 1987, 1988, 1989, 1990, 1991, 1994

Wexford (7): 1968, 1969, 1975, 2007, 2010, 2011, 2012

Antrim (6): 1945, 1946, 1947, 1956, 1967, 1979

Tipperary (5): 1999, 2000, 2001, 2003, 2004

Galway (2): 1996, 2013

CAMOGIE TEAM OF THE CENTURY 2004*

Eileen Duffy-O'Mahony (Dublin), Liz Neary (Kilkenny), Marie Costine-O'Donovan (Cork), Mary Sinnott-Dinan (Wexford), Bridie Martin-McGarry (Kilkenny), Sandie Fitzgibbon (Cork), Margaret O'Leary-Leacy (Wexford), Mairéad McAtamney-Magill (Antrim), Linda Mellerick (Cork), Sophie Brack (Dublin), Kathleen Mills-Hill (Dublin), Una O'Connor (Dublin), Pat Moloney-Lenihan (Cork), Deirdre Hughes (Tipperary) and Angela Downey-Browne (Kilkenny).

* Selected in 2004, by a team of journalists and past Camogie Association members.

CAMOGIE ALL-STAR AWARDS

2004

Aoife Murray (Cork), Suzanne Kelly (Tipperary), Una O'Dwyer (Tipperary), Áine Codd (Wexford), Mary Leacy (Wexford), Ciara Gaynor (Tipperary), Therese Brophy (Tipperary), Kate Kelly (Wexford), Gemma O'Connor (Cork), Jennifer O'Leary (Cork), Máirín McAleenan

(Down), Clare Grogan (Tipperary), Ann Marie Hayes (Galway), Deirdre Hughes (Tipperary) and Sinéad Millea (Kilkenny).

2005

Jovita Delaney (Tipperary), Sinéad Cahalan (Galway), Catherine O'Loughlin (Wexford), Julie Kirwan (Tipperary), Anna Geary (Cork), Mary O'Connor (Cork), Therese Maher (Galway), Gemma O'Connor (Cork), Ciara Lucey (Dublin), Jennifer O'Leary (Cork), Rachel Moloney (Cork), Clare Grogan (Tipperary), Eimear McDonnell (Tipperary), Catherine O'Loughlin (Clare) and Emer Dillon (Cork).

2006

Jovita Delaney (Tipperary), Regina Glynn (Galway), Suzanne Kelly (Tipperary), Rena Buckley (Cork), Philly Fogarty (Tipperary), Mary O'Connor (Cork), Anna Geary (Cork), Gemma O'Connor (Cork), Kate Kelly (Wexford), Joanne Ryan (Tipperary), Briege Corkery (Cork), Jennifer O'Leary (Cork), Imelda Kennedy (Kilkenny), Louise O'Hara (Dublin) and Veronica Curtin (Galway).

2007

Mags Darcy (Wexford), Eimear Brannigan (Dublin), Catherine O'Loughlin (Wexford), Rose Collins (Limerick), Rena Buckley (Cork), Mary Leacy (Wexford), Cathriona Foley (Cork), Gemma O'Connor (Cork), Philly Fogarty (Tipperary), Veronica Curtin (Galway), Aisling Diamond (Derry), Jennifer O'Leary (Cork), Kate Kelly (Wexford), Clare Grogan (Tipperary) and Una Leacy (Wexford).

2008

Aoife Murray (Cork), Cathriona Foley (Cork), Catherine O'Loughlin (Wexford), Trish O'Halloran (Tipperary), Michaela Morkan (Offaly), Sinéad Cahalan (Galway), Gemma O'Connor (Cork), Briege Corkery (Cork), Orla Cotter (Cork), Jessica Gill (Galway), Therese Maher (Galway), Aoife Neary (Kilkenny), Síle Burns (Cork), Rachel Moloney (Cork) and Jane Adams (Antrim).

2009

Aoife Murray (Cork), Regina Glynn (Galway), Cathriona Foley (Cork), Jacqui Frisby (Kilkenny), Ann Marie Hayes (Galway), Mary O'Connor (Cork), Elaine Aylward (Kilkenny), Briege Corkery (Cork), Ann Dalton (Kilkenny), Katie Power (Kilkenny), Gemma O'Connor (Cork), Therese Maher (Galway), Aoife Neary (Kilkenny), Grainne McGoldrick (Derry) and Rachel Moloney (Cork).

2010

Mags D'Arcy (Wexford), Claire O'Connor (Wexford), Catherine O'Loughlin (Wexford), Niamh Kilkenny (Galway), Regina Glynn (Galway), Mary Leacy (Wexford), Anna Geary (Cork), Orla Kilkenny (Galway), Ann Dalton (Kilkenny), Kate Kelly (Wexford), Una Leacy (Wexford), Brenda Hanney (Galway), Katrina Parrock (Wexford), Ursula Jacob (Wexford) and Aislinn Connolly (Galway).

2011

Susan Earner (Galway), Claire O'Connor (Wexford), Catherine O'Loughlin (Wexford), Lorraine Ryan (Galway), Ann Marie Hayes (Galway), Therese Maher (Galway), Anna Geary (Cork), Niamh Kilkenny (Galway), Jill Horan (Tipperary), Kate Kelly (Wexford), Una Leacy (Wexford), Jennifer O'Leary (Cork), Katrina Parrock (Wexford), Ursula Jacob (Wexford) and Brenda Hanney (Galway).

2012

Aoife Murray (Cork), Claire O'Connor (Wexford), Catherine O'Loughlin (Wexford), Sheila O'Sullivan (Offaly), Pamela Mackey (Cork), Gemma O'Connor (Cork), Deirdre Codd (Wexford), Niamh Kilkenny (Galway), Jennifer O'Leary (Cork), Kate Kelly (Wexford), Niamh McGrath (Galway), Briege Corkery (Cork), Katriona Mackey (Cork), Ursula Jacob (Wexford) and Katrina Parrock (Wexford).

2013

Susan Earner (Galway), Mairead Power (Kilkenny), Sarah Dervan (Galway), Lorraine Ryan (Galway), Edwina Keane (Kilkenny), Therese Maher (Galway), Chloe Morey (Clare), Niamh Kilkenny (Galway), Jennifer O'Leary (Cork), Katie Power (Kilkenny), Niamh McGrath (Galway), Kate Kelly (Wexford), Shelly Farrell (Kilkenny), Elaine Dermody (Offaly) and Ailish O'Reilly (Galway).

ALL-IRELAND LADIES SENIOR FOOTBALL CHAMPIONSHIP

- The winning team is presented with the Brendan Martin Cup.
- The Ladies Association was founded in 1974 in Hayes Hotel, Tipperary, where the GAA was born.
- Tipperary man Jim Kennedy was the first president elected.
- Tipperary won the first title in 1974.
- Kerry head the winners' list with eleven championship wins.
- Between 1982 and 1990 Kerry won a record nine titles.
- Ladies' Gaelic football is now also played in the United Kingdom, the United States, Australia, Asia and on mainland Europe.

Roll of Honour

Kerry (11): 1976, 1982, 1983, 1984, 1985, 1986, 1987, 1988, 1989, 1990, 1993

Cork (8): 2005, 2006, 2007, 2008, 2009, 2011, 2012, 2013

Waterford (5): 1991, 1992, 1994, 1995, 1998

Mayo (4): 1999, 2000, 2002, 2003

Tipperary (3): 1974, 1975, 1980

Monaghan (2): 1996, 1997

Offaly (2): 1979, 1981

Cavan (1): 1977

Roscommon (1): 1978

Laois (1): 2001

Galway (1): 2004

Dublin (1): 2010

RECENT ALL-STAR AWARDS

2003

Andrea O'Donoghue (Kerry), Nuala Ó Sé (Mayo), Helena Lohan (Mayo), Maria Kavanagh (Dublin), Anna Lisa Crotty (Waterford), Martina Farrell (Dublin), Emer Flaherty (Galway), Angie McNally (Dublin), Mary O'Donnell (Waterford), Lisa Cohill (Galway), Christina Heffernan (Mayo), Michelle McGing (Mayo), Mary O'Rourke (Waterford), Geraldine O'Shea (Kerry) and Kacey O'Driscoll (Kerry).

2004

Cliodhna O'Connor (Dublin), Christine O'Reilly (Monaghan), Ruth Stephens (Galway), Helena Lohan (Mayo), Rena Buckley (Cork), Louise Keegan (Dublin), Emer Flaherty (Galway), Annette Clarke (Galway), Claire Egan (Mayo), Lisa Cohill (Galway), Bernie Finlay (Dublin), Valerie Mulcahy (Cork), Mary Nevin (Dublin), Geraldine O'Shea (Kerry) and Cora Staunton (Mayo).

2005

Una Carroll (Galway), Ruth Stephens (Galway), Angela Walsh (Cork), Leona Tector (Wexford), Briege Corkery (Cork), Aoibheann Daly (Galway), Gemma Fay (Dublin), Juliet Murphy (Cork), Claire Egan (Mayo), Geraldine Doherty (Meath), Deirdre O'Reilly (Cork), Lyndsey Davey (Dublin), Valerie Mulcahy (Cork), Niamh Fahy (Galway) and Lorna Joyce (Galway).

2006

Katrina Connolly (Sligo), Caoimhe Marley (Armagh), Angela Walsh (Cork), Rena Buckley (Cork), Aoibheann Daly (Galway), Bronagh O'Donnell (Armagh), Patricia Fogarty (Laois), Caroline O'Hanlon (Armagh), Mary O'Donnell (Waterford), Nollaig Cleary (Cork), Gráinne Nulty (Meath), Sarah O'Connor (Kerry), Tracey Lawlor (Laois), Mary O'Connor (Cork) and Dymphna O'Brien (Limerick).

2007

Mary Rose Kelly (Wexford), Rebecca Hallahan (Waterford), Angela Walsh (Cork), Rena Buckley (Cork), Claire O'Hara (Mayo), Brid Stack (Cork), Briege Corkery (Cork), Juliet Murphy (Cork), Brianne Leahy (Kildare), Sarah McLoughlin (Leitrim), Cora Staunton (Mayo), Tracey Lawlor (Laois), Valerie Mulcahy (Cork), Gemma Begley (Tyrone) and Deirdre O'Reilly (Cork).

2008

Elaine Harte (Cork), Linda Barrett (Cork), Angela Walsh (Cork), Sharon Courtney (Monaghan), Briege Corkery (Cork), Brid Stack (Cork), Neamh Woods (Tyrone), Juliet Murphy (Cork), Amanda Casey (Monaghan), Nollaig Cleary (Cork), Niamh Kindlon (Monaghan), Michaela Downey (Down), Edel Byrne (Monaghan), Cora Staunton (Mayo) and Edel Hanley (Tipperary).

2009

Cliodhna O'Connor (Dublin), Noelle Tierney (Mayo), Angela Walsh (Cork), Geraldine O'Flynn (Cork), Briege Corkery (Cork), Martha Carter (Mayo), Siobhan McGrath (Dublin), Juliet Murphy (Cork), Norita Kelly (Cork), Nollaig Cleary (Cork), Edel Byrne (Monaghan), Noelle Earley (Kildare), Clara McAnespie (Monaghan), Sinéad Aherne (Dublin) and Cora Staunton (Mayo).

2010

Edel Murphy (Kerry), Rachel Ruddy (Dublin), Lorraine Muckian (Laois), Sinead McLaughlin (Tyrone), Siobhan McGrath (Dublin), Brid Stack (Cork), Gemma Fay (Dublin), Denise Masterson (Dublin), Tracey Lawlor (Laois), Cathy Donnelly (Tyrone), Gemma Begley (Tyrone), Amy McGuinness (Dublin), Yvonne McMonagle (Donegal), Sinead Aherne (Dublin) and Joline Donnelly (Tyrone).

2011

Irene Munnelly (Meath), Grainne McNally (Monaghan), Sharon Courtney (Monaghan), Deirdre O'Reilly (Cork), Briege Corkery (Cork), Brid Stack (Cork), Geraldine O'Flynn (Cork), Juliet Murphy (Cork), Tracey Lawlor (Laois), Therese McNally (Monaghan), Elaine Kelly (Dublin), Mary Kirwan (Laois), Ciara McAnespie (Monaghan), Rhona Ni Bhuachalla (Cork) and Sinead Aherne (Dublin).

2012

Elaine Harte (Cork), Cait Lynch (Kerry), Brid Stack (Cork), Christina Reilly (Monaghan), Briege Corkery (Cork), Rena Buckley (Cork), Geraldine O'Flynn (Cork), Sinead Goldrick (Dublin), Caroline O'Hanlon (Armagh), Sarah Houlihan (Kerry), Cora Staunton (Mayo), Ciara O'Sullivan (Cork), Cathriona McConnell (Monaghan), Valerie Mulcahy (Cork) and Louise Ní Muircheartaigh (Kerry).

2013

Yvonne Byrne (Mayo), Grainne McNally (Monaghan), Sharon Courtney (Monaghan), Deirdre O'Reilly (Cork), Briege Corkery (Cork), Sinead Goldrick (Dublin), Geraldine O'Flynn (Cork), Annette Clarke (Galway), Juliet Murphy (Cork), Sarah Houlihan (Kerry), Caoimhe Mohan (Monaghan), Cora Courtney (Monaghan), Valerie Mulcahy (Cork), Cora Staunton (Mayo) and Louise Ní Muircheartaigh (Kerry).

THE INTER-PROVINCIAL CHAMPIONSHIP

- This competition is commonly known as the Railway Cup due to the donation of the original trophy by Irish Rail.

- It was first contested in 1927. Munster won the football competition and Leinster won the first hurling title.

- Combined Universities teams competed for two years, winning the football competition in 1973.

- Ulster has never won the hurling competition. The nearest they came was in 1995, when losing by a single point to Munster.

- Since 2001 the tournament has been sponsored by Clare businessman Martin Donnelly.

- The 1927 Munster Railway Cup football side was comprised of the entire Kerry team.

- The 2009 hurling final took place in March in Abu Dhabi in the United Arab Emirates. Abu Dhabi joined a growing list of foreign cities including Boston, Paris and Rome to have hosted the competition.

- Christy Ring, who played during the golden age of the competition, won a record eighteen times with Munster.

ROLL OF HONOUR: HURLING*

Munster (45): 1928, 1929, 1930, 1931, 1934, 1937, 1938, 1939, 1940, 1942, 1943, 1944, 1945, 1946, 1948, 1949, 1950, 1951, 1952, 1953, 1955, 1957, 1958, 1959, 1960, 1961, 1963, 1966, 1968, 1969, 1970, 1976, 1978, 1981, 1984, 1985, 1992, 1995, 1996, 1997, 2000, 2001, 2005, 2007, 2013

Leinster (29): 1927, 1932, 1933, 1935, 1936, 1941, 1954, 1956, 1962, 1964, 1965, 1967, 1971, 1972, 1973, 1974, 1975, 1977, 1979, 1988, 1993, 1998, 2002, 2003, 2006, 2008, 2009, 2012, 2014

Connacht (11): 1947, 1980, 1982, 1983, 1986, 1987, 1989, 1991, 1994, 1999, 2004

* not contested in 1990 and 2010–11

ROLL OF HONOUR: FOOTBALL*

Ulster (31): 1942, 1943, 1947, 1950, 1956, 1960, 1963, 1964, 1965, 1966, 1968, 1970, 1971, 1979, 1980, 1983, 1984, 1989, 1991, 1992, 1993, 1994, 1995, 1998, 2000, 2003, 2004, 2007, 2009, 2012, 2013

Leinster (28): 1928, 1929, 1930, 1932, 1933, 1935, 1939, 1940, 1944, 1945, 1952, 1953, 1954, 1955, 1959, 1961, 1962, 1974, 1985, 1986, 1987, 1988, 1996, 1997, 2001, 2002, 2005, 2006,

Munster (15): 1927, 1931, 1941, 1946, 1948, 1949, 1972, 1975, 1976, 1977, 1978, 1981, 1982, 1999, 2008

Connacht (10): 1934, 1936, 1937, 1938, 1951, 1957, 1958, 1967, 1969, 2014

Combined Universities (1): 1973

* not contested in 1990 and 2010–11

GAA HURLING AND FOOTBALL LEGENDS

HENRY SHEFFLIN (KILKENNY), HURLING

- The game's most decorated player holds a host of championship records. 2012 saw him surpass Christy Ring's haul of eight All-Ireland winners' medals.

- His first taste of the inter-county scene came at the age of seventeen when he first linked up with the Kilkenny minor team, before later lining out with the Under-21 side.

- He made his senior debut in the 1999 championship.

- He has won thirteen Leinster medals and six National Hurling League medals. The All-Ireland-winning captain in 2007, he has also been an All-Ireland runner-up on three occasions.

- He became the top scorer of all time in the 2010 Leinster Hurling final, when overtaking fellow Kilkenny man Eddie Keher. Keher had scored 439 points in total.

- The records continued to tumble in 2012, as he played his fifty-eighth championship match for the 'Cats', taking over from the great D. J. Carey's mark of fifty-seven.

- He is the only player to have scored a goal in fourteen consecutive championship seasons. His record run of sixty-two appearances for the 'black and amber' came to an end against Offaly in Tullamore in 2013.

– 'King Henry's' reign has also included a record-breaking eleven All-Star awards.

– He was chosen as the RTÉ Sports Person of the Year in 2006. He was the only amateur sports personality on the list!

HONOURS

St Kieran's College

– All-Ireland Colleges Senior Hurling Championship (1): 1996

– Leinster Colleges Senior Hurling Championship (2): 1996, 1997

Waterford Institute of Technology

– Fitzgibbon Cup (2): 1998–99, 1999–2000

Ballyhale Shamrocks

– All-Ireland Senior Club Hurling Championship (2): 2007, 2010

– Leinster Senior Club Hurling Championship (3): 2006, 2008, 2009

– Kilkenny Senior Hurling Championship (4): 2006, 2008, 2009, 2012

Kilkenny

- All-Ireland Senior Hurling Championship (9): 2000, 2002, 2003, 2006, 2007, 2008, 2009, 2011, 2012

- Leinster Senior Hurling Championship (13): 1999, 2000, 2001, 2002, 2003, 2005, 2006, 2007, 2008, 2009, 2010, 2011, 2014

- National Hurling League (6): 2002, 2003, 2005, 2006, 2009, 2014

- Walsh Cup (5): 2005, 2006, 2007, 2009, 2014

- Leinster Railway Cup (3): 2002, 2003, 2009

Individual Awards

- Texaco Hurler of the Year (3): 2002, 2006, 2012

- All-Stars Hurler of the Year (3): 2002, 2006, 2012

- GPA Hurler of the Year (2): 2002, 2006

- RTÉ Sports Person of the Year (1): 2006

- All-Stars (11): 2000, 2002, 2003, 2004, 2005, 2006, 2007, 2008, 2009, 2011, 2012

RECORDS

- The only player in the history of Gaelic games to have won nine All-Ireland senior winners' medals on the field of play.

- The only player to score a goal in fourteen consecutive championship seasons (1999–2012).

- Joint winner of the highest total of Leinster Championship titles ever won (13).

- Highest scorer in the history of the All-Ireland championship.

- Highest scoring average in the history of the All-Ireland championship (9 points per game).

- Holds the most All-Star awards of any player (11).

- Holds the most 'Player of the Year' awards (3).

- Highest scorer from play (24–136 = 208 points) in the history of the All-Ireland championship, including the All-Ireland final replay 30/09/2012.

CHRISTY RING (CORK), HURLING

- Christy Ring (12 October 1920–2 March 1979) was born in Cloyne, County Cork.

- Nicknamed 'The Wizard of Cloyne'.

- He arrived on the inter-county scene aged sixteen when he played with the Cork minor team, before later lining out with the junior side.

- He made his senior inter-county debut in 1939.

- Ring represented the Munster Railway Cup team for a record twenty-three consecutive seasons, winning a record eighteen Railway Cup medals. No other player in the history of the competition has broken the double figures barrier in winning medals.

– He won eight All-Ireland medals, nine Munster medals and three National Hurling League medals.

– An All-Ireland runner-up on two occasions, Ring also captained the team to three All-Ireland victories.

– He had a stellar club career, winning thirteen championship medals with Glen Rovers.

– His scoring record stood until the 1970s when it was surpassed by Eddie Keher. His haul of eight All-Ireland medals was a record which stood for over ten years, until it was equalled by John Doyle and subsequently surpassed by Henry Shefflin.

– He contested twenty-three Railway Cup finals in a row, winning eighteen. He scored 4–5 in the 1957 final, five points more than opponents Connacht could muster in total.

– He was named Hurler of the Year just one year shy of his fortieth birthday.

– Ring made sixty-five championship appearances for Cork, more than any other player in the county's history and a national record that stood for nearly fifty years, until it was surpassed by Tipperary net minder Brendan Cummins.

– He left the inter-county scene prior to the start of the 1964 championship.

– He was selected on the Hurling Team of the Century in 1984 and the Hurling Team of the Millennium.

HONOURS

Cork

- All-Ireland Senior Hurling Championship (8): 1941, 1942, 1943, 1944, 1946, 1952, 1953, 1954

- Munster Senior Hurling Championship (9): 1942, 1943, 1944, 1946, 1947, 1952, 1953, 1954, 1956

- National Hurling League (3): 1940, 1941, 1953

Other

- Ring's life was celebrated in the film produced by Gael-Linn in 1964.

- Páirc Uí Rinn in Cork is named in his honour.

- He has been commemorated by a life-size statue in his native village of Cloyne.

- In 2005 the GAA commemorated Ring's great achievements by creating the Christy Ring Cup, a hurling award for the tier two-winning team. The inaugural Christy Ring Cup final was played on Sunday 14 August 2005 between Down and Westmeath.

- The Christy Ring Bridge over the River Lee in Cork city also remembers his achievements.

MICK MACKEY (LIMERICK), HURLING

- Michael 'Mick' Mackey was born on 12 July 1912 and died on 13 September 1982.

- Nicknamed 'The Playboy of the Southern World'.

- He won three All-Ireland medals and five Munster medals.

- He also won five National Hurling League medals.

- Mackey made forty-two championship appearances for Limerick. His retirement came following the conclusion of the 1947 championship.

- Mackey represented the Munster inter-provincial team for twelve years.

- He won eight Railway Cup medals during that period.

- He won fifteen Club Championship medals with Ahane.

HONOURS

Ahane

- Limerick Senior Hurling Championship (15): 1931, 1933, 1934, 1935, 1936, 1937, 1938, 1939, 1942, 1943, 1944, 1945, 1946, 1947, 1948

- Limerick Senior Football Championship (5): 1935, 1936, 1937, 1938, 1939

Limerick

–   All-Ireland Senior Hurling Championship (3): 1934, 1936 (c), 1940 (c)

–   Munster Senior Hurling Championship (5): 1933, 1934, 1935, 1936 (c), 1940 (c)

–   National Hurling League (5): 1934, 1935, 1936 (c), 1937, 1938

Munster

–   Railway Cup (8): 1934, 1937 (c), 1938, 1939, 1940, 1943, 1945, 1946

Individual Honours

–   Hurling Team of the Millennium: Centre-forward

–   Hurling Team of the Century: Centre-forward

–   GAA All-Time All-Star Award: 1980

–   Caltex Hall of Fame Award: 1961

JACK O'SHEA (KERRY), FOOTBALL

–   He hailed from one of Kerry's finest footballing strongholds: Caherciveen. The South Kerry town was home to the great Jack Murphy, Jerome O'Shea and the mercurial Maurice Fitzgerald.

–   He was born on 19 November 1957.

- O'Shea made his senior inter-county debut with Kerry in late 1976 versus Meath in Navan.

- His goal against Offaly in the 1981 All-Ireland final was one of the finest ever seen at the venue.

- He was named Footballer of the Year four times.

- He retired after Kerry's shock defeat to Clare in the 1992 Munster final.

- He was appointed manager of the Mayo Senior team in 1992. In his first year the team won the Connacht title, beating Roscommon.

- He represented St Mary's, 1970s–84; Leixlip, 1985–90s, during his club career.

HONOURS

Kerry

- Munster Senior Football Championship (10): 1977, 1978, 1979, 1980, 1981, 1982, 1984, 1985, 1986, 1991

- All-Ireland Senior Football Championship (7): 1978, 1979, 1980, 1981, 1984, 1985, 1986

- National Football League (3): 1977, 1982, 1984

Individual Honours

- Footballer of the Year (4): 1980, 1981, 1984, 1985

- All-Stars (6): 1980, 1981, 1982, 1983, 1984, 1985

SEAN O'NEILL (DOWN), FOOTBALL

- He was a member of the famous Down team that won consecutive All-Irelands (1960, 1961).

- He won a record eight Railway Cup medals with Ulster.

- He scored eighty-five goals and over 500 points in his Down career.

- He was selected on the first two All-Star teams (1971, 1972).

- He was chosen as right half-forward on the Team of the Millennium, though many would argue that full-forward was his best position.

- Despite featuring on a Down team that was in decline he was still voted Footballer of the Year in 1968.

- He was in scintillating form in 1968, producing outstanding displays in the All-Ireland semi-final and final, as well as scoring a wonder goal in the decider.

HONOURS
Down

- All-Ireland Senior Football Championship (3): 1960, 1961, 1968

- National Football League (3): 1960, 1962, 1968

- Ulster Senior Football Championship (8): 1959, 1960, 1961, 1963, 1965, 1966, 1968, 1971

Ulster

– Railway Cup (8): 1960, 1963, 1964, 1965, 1966, 1968, 1970, 1971

SEÁN PURCELL (GALWAY), FOOTBALL

– Seán Purcell was born on 27 August 1929.

– The Galway great was nicknamed 'The Master'.

– He formed a fearsome partnership with fellow club and county team-mate Frank Stockwell. They were known as the 'Terrible Twins'.

– His footballing career spanned three decades – the 1940s, 1950s and 1960s.

– He played college football with St Jarlath's of Tuam.

– Seán Purcell died at the age of seventy-six on 27 August 2005.

HONOURS

Galway

– All-Ireland Senior Football Championship (1): 1956

– Connacht Senior Football Championship (6): 1954, 1956, 1957, 1958, 1959, 1960

– National Football League (1): 1957

Connacht

– The Railway Cup (3): 1951, 1957, 1958

Tuam Stars

– Galway Senior Football Championship (10): 1947, 1952, 1954, 1955, 1956, 1957, 1958, 1959, 1960, 1962

ALL-IRELAND MINOR AND UNDER-21 CHAMPIONSHIP

UNDER-21 HURLING

–   The Bord Gáis Energy GAA Hurling Under-21 All-Ireland Championship was created in 1964.

–   The 2006 final went to a replay after a last gasp Kilkenny goal earned a 2–14 to 2–14 draw. The 'Cats' won the replay against Tipperary 1–11 to 0–11.

–   Clare won the 2013 All-Ireland with most of their under-21-winning team from 2012.

–   The 2012 under-21-winning team scored a dramatic stoppage time goal in that year's Munster final to thwart Tipperary.

–   When Tipperary won the first championship in 1964 they scored a massive total of forty goals and thirty-nine points.

–   Cork in the past were the most successful team in the championship with their four-in-a-row from 1968–71.

–   The most notable feat in recent years was the Limerick three-in-a-row between 2000 and 2002.

–   The treble of winning senior, under-21 and minor titles in the same year has been achieved by Cork in 1970 and by Kilkenny in 1975 and 2003.

– Kilkenny repeated that feat in 2008 and also won the intermediate championship, becoming the first county in the history of the GAA to win all four major championships in a single year.

– In 2009 Clare won their first ever All-Ireland under-21 title with a 0–15 to 0–14 win over Kilkenny at Croke Park.

Roll of Honour

Kilkenny (11): 1974, 1975, 1977, 1984, 1990, 1994, 1999, 2003, 2004, 2006, 2008

Cork (11): 1966, 1968, 1969, 1970, 1971, 1973, 1976, 1982, 1988, 1997, 1998

Galway (10): 1972, 1978, 1983, 1986, 1991, 1993, 1996, 2005, 2007, 2011

Tipperary (9): 1964, 1967, 1979, 1980, 1981, 1985, 1989, 1995, 2010

Limerick (4): 1987, 2000, 2001, 2002

Clare (3): 2009, 2012, 2013

Waterford (1): 1992

Wexford (1): 1965

UNDER-21 FOOTBALL

– The prize for the winning team is the Clarke Cup, which is named in honour of former Kildare Secretary and Treasurer Tim Clarke.

- Kerry have contested the most finals. They have reached the decider on seventeen occasions.

- Cadbury have become the main sponsors of the competition in recent times. They introduced a special award known as 'The Cadbury's Hero of the Future' aimed at identifying upcoming future football stars.

- A number of 'Heroes' have gone on to grace the Senior code. Rory O'Carroll, who won the 2010 award, starred at full-back as 'The Dubs' reclaimed the Sam Maguire, ending a sixteen-year drought with victory over Kerry in 2011.

- Cork are the most successful team in the history of the Under-21 Championship.

- Two teams have achieved three-in-a-rows: Kerry from 1975–77 and Cork from 1984–86.

- Laois contested the first ever final in 1964, losing to Kerry. They had to wait thirty-four years to reach their second decider. Sadly lightning struck twice as the Kingdom won again, on a scoreline of 2–8 to 0–11.

- Cavan have reached three deciders, in 1988, 1996 and 2011, losing on all three occasions.

- The coveted treble of winning senior, under-21 and minor titles in the same year has been achieved on just one occasion, by Kerry in 1975.

Roll of Honour

Cork (11): 1970, 1971, 1980, 1981, 1984, 1985, 1986, 1989, 1994, 2007, 2009

Kerry (10): 1964, 1973, 1975, 1976, 1977, 1990, 1995, 1996, 1998, 2008

Galway (5): 1972, 2002, 2005, 2011, 2013

Mayo (4): 1967, 1974, 1983, 2006

Tyrone (4): 1991, 1992, 2000, 2001

Dublin (3): 2003, 2010, 2012

Roscommon (2): 1966, 1978

Derry (2): 1968, 1997

Donegal (2): 1982, 1987

Kildare (1): 1965

Down (1): 1979

Meath (1): 1993

Offaly (1): 1988

Westmeath (1): 1999

Antrim (1): 1969

Armagh (1): 2004

MINOR HURLING

- The 'Big Three' of Cork, Kilkenny and Tipperary are the most dominant teams in minor hurling.

- The tournament was created in 1928 and the winners receive The Irish Press Cup.

- The title has been won by ten different teams, nine of which have won the title more than once.

- Offaly won their first title in 1986, and went on to win three titles in four years (1986, 1987, 1989).

- Tipperary's three-goal All-Ireland hero Lar Corbett never played minor for his county.

- Kilkenny, Cork and Tipperary have claimed famous three-in-a-rows over the years.

- Joe Dunphy of Mooncoin is the only player to captain a county team to two successive All-Ireland minor titles. He achieved this honour with Kilkenny in 1961 and 1962.

- Eight-time All-Ireland medal winner Eddie Brennan of Kilkenny never played minor hurling for his county.

- Clare won their only All-Ireland Minor Championship in 1997.

Roll of Honour*

Kilkenny (20): 1931, 1935, 1936, 1950, 1960, 1961, 1962, 1972, 1973, 1975, 1977, 1981, 1988, 1990, 1991, 1993, 2002, 2003, 2008, 2010

Tipperary (19): 1930, 1932, 1933, 1934, 1947, 1949, 1952, 1953, 1955, 1956, 1957, 1959, 1976, 1980, 1982, 1996, 2006, 2007, 2012

Cork (18): 1928, 1937, 1938, 1939, 1941, 1951, 1964, 1967, 1969, 1970, 1971, 1974, 1978, 1979, 1985, 1995, 1998, 2001

Galway (9): 1983, 1992, 1994, 1999, 2000, 2004, 2005, 2009, 2011

Dublin (4): 1945, 1946, 1954, 1965

Offaly (3): 1986, 1987, 1989

Limerick (3): 1940, 1958, 1984

Wexford (3): 1963, 1966, 1968

Waterford (3): 1929, 1948, 2013

Clare (1): 1997

* not contested in 1942–44

MINOR FOOTBALL CHAMPIONSHIP

- The prize for the winning team is the Tom Markham Cup, which is named in honour of a prominent former member of Clare GAA.

- The first minor championship was played in 1929 when Clare were crowned the champions, defeating Longford.

- Munster head the provincial Roll of Honour, with twenty-four wins in the competition. Leinster are next with twenty-one, followed closely by Ulster's twenty.

- The last win by a Munster team was Tipperary in 2011, seventy-seven years after their previous win in 1934.

- Kerry and Dublin are the most successful teams in minor football, closely followed by Cork. All three teams have achieved three-in-a-rows: Kerry from 1931–33; Cork from 1967–69; and Dublin from 1954–56.

– Westmeath won a rare All-Ireland for the county when they upstaged Derry 1–10 to 0–11 in 1995.

– Former Kerry great Eoin 'Bomber' Liston never played minor football for the Kingdom.

– Despite winning ten championships, and lying a close second on the all-time Roll of Honour, Cork's last success in this grade was thirteen years ago, in 2000.

Roll of Honour*

Kerry (11): 1931, 1932, 1933, 1946, 1950, 1962, 1963, 1975, 1980, 1988, 1994

Dublin (11): 1930, 1945, 1954, 1955, 1956, 1958, 1959, 1979, 1982, 1984, 2012

Cork (10): 1961, 1967, 1968, 1969, 1972, 1974, 1981, 1991, 1993, 2000

Tyrone (8): 1947, 1948, 1973, 1998, 2001, 2004, 2008, 2010

Mayo (7): 1935, 1953, 1966, 1971, 1978, 1985, 2013

Galway (6): 1952, 1960, 1970, 1976, 1986, 2007

Down (4): 1977, 1987, 1999, 2005

Roscommon (4): 1939, 1941, 1951, 2006

Derry (4): 1965, 1983, 1989, 2002

Laois (3): 1996, 1997, 2003

Meath (3): 1957, 1990, 1992

Tipperary (2): 1934, 2011

Louth (2): 1936, 1940

Cavan (2): 1937, 1938

Armagh (2): 1949, 2009

Offaly (1): 1964

Westmeath (1): 1995

Clare (1): 1929

* not contested in 1942–44

GAA HANDBALL

- Handball is also played in the USA, Canada, Australia, Mexico and Spain.

- The first record of handball was in 1789, when Thomas 'Buck' Whalley won a wager of 100 guineas for playing handball against the walls of Jerusalem.

- William Baggs of Tipperary became the first recognised champion in the 1870s.

- The Irish Handball Council came into existence in 1924.

- The first World Championship took place in 1964.

- RTÉ's *Top Ace* television tournament was played for the first time in 1973.

- The early years of the World Championships were dominated by American players.

- That stranglehold was broken by Cavan man Paul Brady in October 2003.

- Fiona Shannon of Antrim won the singles title on the same day, to make it an Irish double.

- D. J. Carey won All-Ireland doubles titles with fellow Kilkenny man and handball legend, Michael 'Ducksy' Walsh (despite variations, Ducksy is what Michael uses).

- Handball was re-branded to GAA Handball in 2009.

HANDBALL GREATS

Michael 'Ducksy' Walsh (Kilkenny)

- The small council estate in Kilkenny city, where this All-Ireland softball singles champion was born has produced an amazing six All-Ireland champions!

- He won thirty-eight All-Ireland senior softball titles, split between singles and doubles.

- He joined the Talbot's Inch Club and was All-Ireland Under-12 champion by the age of ten.

- Talbot's Inch Club in Kilkenny is one of the oldest in Ireland and has produced over 100 Senior All-Ireland medal-winners. It was opened by President W. T. Cosgrave in July 1928.

- Ducksy won his first softball Irish singles title in 1985. It sparked an astonishing run of sixteen singles and doubles titles in seventeen years, thirteen of these in a row.

- He formed a fearsome doubles combination with fellow Kilkenny man Eugene Downey.

- He won three All-Ireland softball doubles titles with hurling legend D. J. Carey.

- His longevity was rubber stamped in recent years, by yet another All-Ireland Singles semi-final appearance. There he faced fellow Kilkenny man Michael Gregan, seventeen years his junior!

– He was inducted into the Leinster GAA Hall of Fame in 2003.

Senior All-Ireland Singles (winning years): 1986, 1987, 1988, 1989, 1990, 1991, 1996, 1998

Paul Brady (Cavan)

– He won his first All-Ireland senior title in March 2003. He defeated Tony Healy from Cork 21–18 to 21–6 in the best of three decider at O'Loughlin's, Kilkenny. In the same tournament he added the doubles title, with Michael Finnegan, against Meath.

– In October 2003 he won the first of four World Open Singles titles.

– Brady was called into the Cavan senior football panel by Mattie Kerrigan in the winter of 2002.

– Brady's uncle was the great 'Gunner' Brady, who played for Cavan for many years, winning three All-Ireland medals.

– In the final of the Ultimate Handball Showdown in Seattle in 2004 Brady comfortably defeated Californian David Chapman to win the first prize of $50,000, still the richest purse in the sport's history.

– He won four World titles in a row: 2003, 2006, 2009 and 2012.

–   In defeating Mexican-born Luis Moreno, who is nicknamed 'The Natural', in the 2012 decider, he affirmed his status as one of the greatest players in handball history.

Senior All-Ireland Singles (winning years): 2003, 2005, 2006, 2007, 2008, 2009, 2010, 2011, 2012, 2013

WIT AND WISDOM OF THE GAA

Mícheál Ó Muircheartaigh alludes to what most of us feared already, that spirituality and Sligo success in football don't go hand in hand:

> 'I saw a few Sligo people at Mass in Gardiner Street this morning and the omens seem to be good for them. The priest was wearing the same colours as the Sligo jersey! Forty yards out on the Hogan Stand side of the field Ciarán Whelan goes on a rampage, it's a goal. So much for religion.'

Brian Cody sends a chilling message to the hurling fraternity:

> 'We are not gone, and if anyone says we are gone, we will bloody well show them.'

Christy Ring suggests that player welfare is not all that it should be:

> 'Small cut, big bandage, big cut, no bandage.'

Ger Loughnane displays his love of Tipperary!

> 'I'm not giving away any secrets like that to Tipperary. If I had my way, I wouldn't even tell them the time of the throw-in.'

Cyril Farrell on *The Sunday Game*, waxing lyrical about Lar Corbett's pace:

> 'He's like Ben Bolt.'

Des Cahill, *The Sunday Game* host, in riposte to the ex-Galway manager's utterance:

> 'Is that Usain Bolt's brother?'

Ger Loughnane on Dublin's championship opener against Wexford in 2013:

> 'They played constipated hurling.'

John O'Mahony gives an insight into the distinction between victory and defeat:

> 'Whenever a team loses, there's always a row at half-time, but when they win, it's an inspirational speech.'

Pat Spillane gives an expert view on 'puke' football:

> 'The first half was even, the second half was even worse.'

Michael O'Hehir puts the hex on Kerry's 1982 five-in-a-row bid, and as a result Seamus Darby wins the freedom of Offaly:

> 'Is there a goal in this game?'

Pete McGrath, Down manager, attempts to rationalise the All-Ireland football champions bout of 'second season syndrome':

'Loss of appetite comes like a thief in the night.'

Mícheál Ó Muircheartaigh on the GAA's version of the Tortoise and the Hare!

'Pat Fox has it on his hurley and is motoring well now. But here comes Joe Rabbitte hot on his tail. I've seen it all now – a Rabbitte chasing a Fox around Croke Park!'

Christy Ring gives Nostradamus a run for his money, as he predicts hurling's brave new world:

'My hurling days are over, but let no one say that the best hurlers belong to the past. They are here with us now and better yet to come.'

Mícheál Ó Muircheartaigh feels right at home in the heart of New York:

'And Brian Dooher is down injured. And while he is I'll tell ye a little story. I was in Times Square in New York last week, and I was missing the Championship back home. So I approached a news stand and I said: "I suppose ye wouldn't have *The Kerryman*, would ye?" To which the Egyptian behind the counter turned to me and said: "Do you want the North Kerry edition or the South Kerry edition?" He had both. So I bought both. And Dooher is back on his feet.'

Celebrated commentator Michael O'Hehir gets all geometrical!

> 'And it looks like there's a bit of a schemozzle in the parallelogram.'

Joe Brolly on the raw beauty of team-mate Geoffrey McGonagle's solo runs:

> 'I was following Geoffrey McGonagle, he had an arse like a bag of cement.'

Tommy Carr gets a dose of replay-itis, as the Dublin-Meath saga enters its fourth instalment:

> 'You would almost wish someone, anyone, would end it. It's gone beyond a joke.'

RTÉ pundit Colm O'Rourke never heard the one about revenge being a dish best served cold:

> 'I will eat my hat if Tyrone win an All-Ireland with Brian Dooher in the team.'

Former Tipperary manager Michael Keating before receiving the latter from the Premier county board:

> 'A clap on the back is only about two feet from a kick in the arse.'

Offaly midfielder Johnny Pilkington on how they cheated on their hurling exams:

'We heard one of the Kilkenny players saying they were going to give us a lesson. Fortunately for us, we were thick at school.'

Mícheál Ó Muircheartaigh on the Ó hAilpín family tree:

'Seán Óg Ó hAilpín ... his father's from Fermanagh, his mother's from Fiji, neither a hurling stronghold.'

Clare FM's Matthew McMahon seeks divine intervention at half-time during the 1995 Munster final:

'Oh Jesus, Mary and Joseph, are we ever going to last?'

Mícheál Ó Muircheartaigh smashes the myth that all of Cork's hurling McCarthys are related:

'Teddy McCarthy to John McCarthy, no relation, John McCarthy back to Teddy McCarthy, still no relation.'

Ex-Tipperary great Tony Wall on how to be creative with your hurley:

'In this environment every boy carries a hurley. He uses it for hunting home the cows, for shooting Indians, for chasing the cat, but above all for hurling.'

REELING IN THE GAA YEARS

GAA FOUNDED IN THURLES, 1 NOVEMBER 1884

Michael Cusack convened the first meeting of the 'Gaelic Athletic Association for the Preservation and Cultivation of National Pastimes'. Maurice Davin was elected as the first president. GAA founder Cusack chose the date to mark the mythical Battle of Cath Gabhra in AD 294, where the legendary Fianna lost their powers.

1887: THE FIRST ALL-IRELAND HURLING FINAL

The first All-Ireland final was held in Birr, County Offaly, on 1 April 1887. While six teams entered the championship, only five took part. Dublin (Metropolitans) could not fulfil their fixture against Tipperary, who received a walkover. Teams consisted of twenty-one players and the games were played on a bigger pitch than today's. Tipperary, represented by Thurles, defeated Galway, represented by Meelick, in the final.

1888: THE FIRST ALL-IRELAND FOOTBALL FINAL

Limerick (Commercials) beat Louth (Young Irelands) to win the first All-Ireland football final. Although this was the 1887 final, the match was not played until 29 April 1888 in Clonskeagh. The rules of the day meant that a goal out-weighed any number of points. The final score was 1–4 to 0–3.

GAA SPLIT

A political split formed within the early GAA, with one faction supporting the militaristic republican IRB, and the other the moderate Irish Parliamentary Party. Matters came to a head at the 1887 Annual Congress as IRB candidate Edward Bennett defeated Maurice Davin in the vote for the presidency. A rival Athletic Association was formed, as the sides could not agree on how to work together. Archbishop Croke brought both sides together, and at a Special Congress in January 1888, Maurice Davin was re-elected as president of the GAA.

1888: THE AMERICAN INVASION TOUR

It was agreed to launch a revival of an ancient tournament, the Tailteann Games. The GAA agreed to host the games in Dublin in 1889. In 1888 Irish athletes embarked on a fund-raising tour of Irish centres in America, staging exhibition displays of hurling and athletics, and international contests between Ireland and America. The tour was not a financial success, but it did arouse interest in Gaelic Games among the Irish and Irish-Americans.

1913: THE PURCHASE OF CROKE PARK

At the 1905 Annual Convention it was decided to erect a memorial in honour of Archbishop Thomas William Croke, the first patron of the GAA, who died in 1902. In 1913 a 'Croke Memorial Tournament' (hurling and football) was held, which resulted in a profit of £1,872 to be used for the memorial. These funds allowed the GAA to purchase Jones Road Sports Ground from Frank Dineen for £3,500. The grounds were then re-named 'Croke Park' in honour of the late Archbishop.

1918: GAELIC SUNDAY

In 1918 the British authorities ordered that no hurling or football games would be allowed unless a special permit was obtained from Dublin Castle. The GAA refused to comply with this decision. At a meeting on 20 July it was unanimously agreed that no such permit would be applied for under any circumstances. Any person applying for a permit, or any player playing in a match in which a permit had been obtained, would automatically be suspended from the association.

In a further act of defiance to the controversial order, the council organised a series of matches for Sunday 4 August 1918. Matches were openly played throughout the country with an estimated 54,000 members taking part. This became known as Gaelic Sunday.

1920: BLOODY SUNDAY

Dublin football team was scheduled to play Tipperary, in Croke Park, on 21 November 1920. The proceeds of the match were to be donated to the Irish Republican Prisoners' Fund. Early on the morning before the game, Michael Collins sent his 'Squad' to assassinate the 'Cairo Gang', a group of undercover British agents working and living in Dublin. A number of shootings took place, leaving fourteen members of the British forces dead. In reprisal the British military entered Croke Park that afternoon and opened fire, killing fourteen people, including one of the players.

THE 1924 TAILTEANN GAMES

With the end of the Civil War, the Irish Free State Government decided to stage the Tailteann Games. The games had been due to take place in 1922, but were postponed on the outbreak of the Civil War. The GAA was given a grant of £10,000 to refurbish Croke Park for the event, out of which they built a new stand, the Hogan Stand.

1939–45: THE GAA AND THE SECOND WORLD WAR

The Second World War started on Sunday 3 September 1939, when war was declared on Germany by Britain, France and their allies. Despite the disruption and uncertainty caused by these events, the 1939 All-Ireland hurling final took place in Croke Park on the same day. Travel and fuel restrictions during the Second World War severely disrupted the playing of Gaelic games. The GAA in Britain continued to play their championships against all the odds.

1947: POLO GROUNDS FINAL

The 1947 All-Ireland senior football final between Cavan and Kerry was a historic first for the GAA. It was played in the Polo Grounds, New York, to stimulate interest in Gaelic Games amongst the Irish-American population there. The final was a titanic battle, with Cavan victorious.

The trip was a public relations triumph, with new clubs formed throughout America. The association also recorded a profit of close to £10,000.

1958: WEMBLEY STAGES GAA

The British GAA paid a rent for Wembley Stadium with the view to hosting an exhibition of Gaelic Games. This venture was so successful that 'Wembley at Whit' became an integral part of the British GAA's calendar until 1975. In 1962 over 40,000 spectators attended the challenge game.

1962: GAA AND TELEFÍS ÉIREANN

Gaelic Games were televised live for the first time. Any concerns that the broadcasting of GAA matches would result in a serious drop in attendances proved unfounded.

1970: FIRST EIGHTY-MINUTE FINAL

Playing time was increased to 80 minutes (from 60) and Kerry won the first 80-minute All-Ireland football final. They defeated Meath by 2–19 to 0–18. Cork won the hurling, with a 6–21 to 5–10 win over Wexford.

1971: RULE 27 IS RESCINDED

At a historic Annual Congress, held in Ulster for the first time, the GAA removed 'Rule 27' from its Official Guide. Members of the association are now permitted to play and attend previously banned international sports like soccer and rugby.

1975: FIRST SEVENTY-MINUTE FINAL

Playing time was reduced to 70 minutes in both codes. Kilkenny took the hurling crown by defeating Galway. Kerry won the football final, with a 2–12 to 0–11 victory over Dublin.

1984: GAA CENTENARY YEAR

The All-Ireland hurling final was played in Thurles, Co. Tipperary, birthplace of the GAA. Cork triumphed over Offaly.

1991: JERSEY SPONSORSHIP IS INTRODUCED

The GAA allowed sponsors' names and logos on players shirts for the first time in its history. Also in this year the Leinster Championship produced an epic first-round battle between Dublin and Meath. The marathon series of four games attracted a total attendance of just under a quarter of a million people.

2001: GAA RULE 21

The controversial rule, which prevented members of the

British Security forces from becoming members of the association, was abolished.

2003: THE NEW CROKE PARK

The newly renovated stadium, with a capacity of 82,300 was opened. It is now one of the finest sporting venues on the planet.

2005: GAA RULE 42

The rule which prevented sports other than Gaelic Games from being played at GAA venues was temporarily suspended. The measure was put in place to allow the Irish rugby team and the Republic of Ireland soccer team to play games at Croke Park while the Lansdowne Road rugby grounds were being redeveloped. Crowds of over 80,000 people attended the All-Ireland hurling finals for the first time since 1956.

2007: FIRST RUGBY GAME

The first rugby international to be held in Croke Park was played between Ireland and France as part of the Six Nations championship. The first soccer international at the venue was a friendly between Ireland and Wales.

2009: ANNIVERSARY

The GAA celebrated its 125th year in existence with an array of events.

2013: THE FIRST FLOODLIT ALL-IRELAND

Saturday 28 September was the date for the 2013 All-Ireland hurling final replay between Cork and Clare. The throw-in was set for 5 p.m. Due to the late start the lights were switched on for the first time for an All-Ireland final. Clare took home the Liam MacCarthy Cup, on a 5–16 to 3–16 scoreline.

REFERENCES

BOOKS AND MAGAZINES

Bellew, Ronnie, *GAA: The Glory Years* (Hodder Headline, 2005)

Corry, Eoghan, *The GAA Book of Lists* (Hodder Headline, 2005)

Ó hEithir, Breandán, *Over the Bar: A Personal Relationship with the GAA* (Collins, 2005)

Ryan, Eddie, in *Ireland's Own*, June, July 2013

Sweeney, Eamon, *Gaelic Sport* (O'Brien, 2004)

WEBSITES

www.allgreatquotes.com
www.bbc.co.uk
www.connachtgaa.ie
www.gaa.ie
www.he.gaa.ie
www.hoganstand.com
www.hurlingstats.com
www.kilkennygaa.ie
www.leinstergaa.ie
www.munstergaa.ie
www.premierview.ie
www.stkieranscollege.ie
www.ulstergaa.ie
www.wikipedia.org